The Great
WINGS
BOOK

The Great

WINGS

BOOK

Hugh Carpenter
& Teri Sandison

CHARTWELL
BOOKS, INC.

To our longtime publisher, patron, and friend, Phil Wood

This edition published in 2011 by
CHARTWELL BOOKS, INC.
A division of BOOK SALES, INC.
276 Fifth Avenue Suite 206
New York, New York 10001
USA

Published by arrangement with
Ten Speed Press,
an imprint of the Crown Publishing Group,
a division of Random House, Inc.

Cover and text design by Katy Brown

Library of Congress Cataloging-in-Publication Data
Carpenter, Hugh.
  The great wings book / Hugh Carpenter & Teri Sandison.
    p. cm.
  Summary: "A collection of 50 chicken wing recipes covering
Pan-Asian, Pan-Latin, and all-American flavors"—Provided
by publisher.
  Includes index.
  ISBN-13: 978-0-7858-2859-4
  1. Cookery (Chicken) 2. Cookery, American. 3. Cookery,
International. I. Sandison, Teri. II. Title.
  TX750.5.C45C36 2008
  641.6'65—dc22
                                    2007039409

Printed in China

10 9 8 7 6 5 4 3

CONTENTS

GREAT WINGS NOW AND FOREVER

This is a cookbook for anyone who feels passionately about chicken wings, whether you are famous for a wing recipe or an untested cook who orders chicken wings at every restaurant. Chicken wings are inexpensive, rich tasting, and easy to cook, and they reheat beautifully. The wing bones distribute the heat and contribute a wonderful sweetness to the meat, while the skin gradually becomes crisp and protects the meat from ever becoming dry.

Until October 30, 1964, chicken wings were thrown away or used for making stock. But on that fortunate, stormy night in Buffalo, New York, home cook Teressa Bellissimo faced pleas from her son, Dominic, and his teenage friends, who were desperately hungry. With nothing available but a package of chicken wings, Teressa went to work, frying the wings and then dipping them in a sauce of melted butter, cayenne pepper, white vinegar, garlic, and salt. What a triumph of great taste. Boys talk, especially about Mom's food, and within months the fad for "Buffalo Chicken Wings" swept the nation.

Since then, according to the National Chicken Council, wing sales have soared. In 2006, 11 billion chicken wings, weighing 2.2 billion pounds, were eaten! Of that, restaurants sold 7.5 billion and markets sold 3.5 billion. Chicken wing sales are strong throughout the year and across the country, although there is a frenzy of chicken wing eating on Super Bowl Sunday, when 450 million wings are consumed.

Chicken wing lovers are everywhere. Every connoisseur knows the ideal cooking method, a secret blend of seasonings, and where to find the best wings served by restaurants. These recipes take just minutes to prepare and require no obscure products, and all the sauces and marinades can be made days in advance.

MENU PLANNING

Chicken wings are most commonly served as an appetizer. Requiring nimble fingers and a willingness to overlook an occasional drip on clothing and surrounding surfaces, we serve wings accompanied by lots of paper napkins and little appetizer plates. Since most wings involve last-minute cooking, it's best to choose surrounding appetizers that are served chilled or at room temperature. Then you can concentrate on the main task: serving wings that will become the source of your culinary legend. Each recipe in this book makes enough wings to serve eight to twelve people as an appetizer.

Wings are also fantastic served as an entrée. Since most of the wing recipes in this book take no longer than 20 minutes of preparation, we like to serve three different wing recipes for a gathering of our friends. Pick wings that use the same cooking technique (such as all roasted, or all barbecued, or all braised), and pick a wing recipe from each of the book's three chapters. That way, you'll have three dramatically different-tasting wing dishes. Three wing recipes will serve eight to twelve (depending on appetite!) as the entrée. Choose as the surrounding dishes all the same foods that would accompany burgers or ribs, such as potato salad, coleslaw, corn on the cob, garlic bread, Caesar salad, apple pie, and ice cream. Exhibit your surgical skills by using a knife and fork, or abandon this in favor of a handier approach. Have fun!

GREAT
PREPARATION
AND COOKING
TECHNIQUES

GREAT TIPS FOR BUYING AND STORING WINGS

Chicken wings are usually sold in packages ranging from 10 to 24. Always keep the wings refrigerated until ready to be cooked. Use by the date on the package. Chicken wings sold by the piece should be cooked within four days.

Each recipe in this book specifies 24 wings. They will weigh about 5 pounds. Most recipes call for discarding the wing tips, called "flappers" by the poultry industry. When the wing tips are removed, the wings are easier to move and take up less room during cooking. But if you love nibbling on the wing tips, leave them attached.

It is unnecessary to rinse the chicken wings with cold water. Washing chicken wings will not eliminate all potential bacteria that may (or may not) be present on the surface of the wings. However, the heat will kill possible bacteria, such as salmonella. Far more important in terms of food safety is smell. Discard any chicken wings that have *any* smell, as this is an indication that the wings have begun to spoil. At this point, rinsing the wings will not protect anyone from food-borne illness.

Always wash your hands, cutting boards, knives, and anything else that comes into contact with raw chicken in hot soapy water.

Fresh Versus Frozen

It's a Tie! Unlike most foods, which are adversely affected when frozen, chicken wings are indestructible! Don't hesitate for a moment if all that is available at the market are frozen wings. They'll still be delicious. If frozen, defrost overnight in the refrigerator. To speed defrosting, submerge the package in a large bowl of cold water, changing the water once an hour. When nearly defrosted, open the package and separate the wings. Once frozen wings have been thawed, never refreeze them.

Reheating

Chicken wings reheat wonderfully for all cooking techniques (grilling, smoking, roasting, and braising), except those that are deep-fried. To reheat, place wings on a shallow baking pan lined with foil, and place in a preheated 300°F oven for 15 minutes. Small amounts of wings can be reheated in a microwave oven.

Marinating Secrets for Great Wings

All these wing recipes taste delicious just rubbed with the marinade and then cooked immediately. But they are even more delicious marinated in the refrigerator for at least 1 hour, and the flavor of the wings will improve if marinated in the refrigerator for 8 to 24 hours. This is also true if the wings are rubbed with a dry rub. When marinating chicken wings, turn them occasionally to ensure that they are evenly coated.

Trimming And Cutting Whole Wings

Chicken wings often have extra skin dangling from the end. Trim this off and discard.

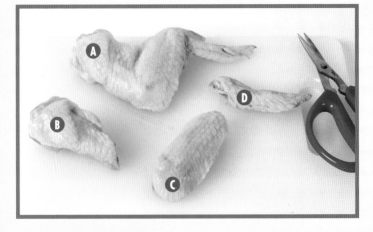

A. Whole wing, open
B. Drummette
C. Middle section
D. Wing tip (the "flapper")

HOW TO LOLLIPOP CHICKEN WINGS

The Chinese have perfected a magical preparation technique for chicken wings. It's an example of their culinary ingenuity of taking a "throwaway" food and transforming it into an elegant form. Once the wings are lollipopped, they are either dipped into a batter and deep-fried (page 120) or rubbed with a marinade/barbecue sauce and oven-roasted (page 119). Supermarket chicken wings, called "drummettes," are just the lower section of the wing and have not been lollipopped, nor can they be lollipopped. You will need the whole wing, including the wing tip.

Hint: This takes practice to perfect. Buy 30 to 40 wings, because there will be a high attrition rate at the outset. Use failed attempts to make homemade chicken broth or one of the braised dishes in this book.

To lollipop the large end (the drumstick part) of the wing:

1. Hold the middle section with your left hand.

2. Hold the drummette with your right hand. Exerting pressure with your right thumb, pop the bone out of the socket. If the socket stays attached to the bone, the chicken wing cannot be lollipopped.

3. Trim off the middle section of the wing.

4. Using your right hand, push the meat on the wing downward to form a neat ball.

5. Using a knife, trim off any skin not attached to the meat.

To lollipop the middle section of the wing:

1. With your left hand, stand the end of the wing on a cutting board.

2. Grip the wing tip with your right hand.

3. With your right hand, push the wing tip "backward" and straight down, exerting maximum downward pressure from the inner arch of your thumb and index finger. Two little wing bones should "pop" free. If they don't, then this section of the wing cannot be lollipopped.

4. Hold the end of the wing in your left hand. With your right hand, grab the smaller bone of the two, and wiggle it around in a circular motion. It should "pop" free.

5. Using your right hand, push the meat on the wing bone downward to form a neat ball.

6. Using a knife, trim off any excess skin not attached to the meat. Repeat the lollipopping technique with the next 99 wings. Rest.

HOW TO PREPARE
WINGS FOR STUFFING

Stuffed chicken wings are a Thai technique that offers the home cook many exciting variations. Stuffing chicken wings is "way easier" to do than lollipopping! It's only the center section of the chicken wing that is stuffed. Nevertheless, you'll need the whole chicken wing with the tip attached (the tip becomes the handle), a sharp paring knife, and a pastry bag to use for piping the filling into the hollow. Note: You can lollipop the bottom section and stuff the middle portion of the wing.

1. Cut off the bottom (drummette) section of the chicken wing.

2. Using a sharp paring knife, cut through the skin and meat around the two end bones.

3. Now make a shallow cut between the two end bones, separating them slightly, but not cutting so deeply that the skin is pierced.

4. Using your thumb and index finger, push the meat/skin away from both bones until both bones are completely exposed.

GREAT PREPARATION AND COOKING TECHNIQUES

5. Grab the end of the little wing and move it in a circular motion until it "pops" free. Repeat this technique with the larger bone.

6. Make one of the fillings. Place this in a pastry bag that has no pastry tip inserted.

7. Insert the pastry bag tip into the wing. Pipe in the filling.

GRILLING

Grilled chicken wings are one of life's great taste sensations. With a little attention and low heat, wings taste moist and acquire an addictive and complex barbecue flavor.

Key equipment is a gas or a charcoal-fired grill large enough to hold the wings. You'll need to have a tight-fitting lid, because wings are always cooked covered to trap in all the smoky essences.

We also recommend spring-loaded tongs, heatproof mitts to protect your hands, and basting brushes made with natural hair or silicon (not nylon, which melts).

In terms of heat source, if you have a nongas barbecue, we recommend using charcoal briquettes, which start easily, provide a steady heat, and are available at every market. Lump hardwood charcoal and hardwood, such as oak, provide superior flavor; however, these burn very hot and fast, and are more likely to burn the food. Use these only if you are a barbecue pro.

Keep the heat low—the skin on chicken wings burns easily. If using a charcoal fire, push the coals out around the periphery of the grill. For gas grills, use just the outside burners, and keep these on medium to low. The heat is at the right temperature if, when you place your hand spread open about 3 inches above the fire, you're forced to remove your hand from the heat at the count of "1001, 1002, 1003."

Regulate the temperature by raising or lowering the gas flame or, with charcoal fires, opening or closing the vents. Remember, it's always better to err on the side of too low a heat (the wings just take longer to cook) than too high a heat (the wings may be badly burned). Be sure to insert an oven thermometer into one of the vents on the top lid.

QUICK GRILLING DIRECTIONS

Marinate, then grill the wings "open" (see page 3, figure A) for even cooking. The key is that lower heat is always better than higher heat. If using a gas barbecue, preheat to medium (325°F). If using charcoal or wood, prepare a fire. When the coals or wood are ash covered, push the coals to the outside of the grill (this is called "the indirect method of grilling"). Brush the cooking grate with flavorless oil, and then lay the wings on the barbecue cooking grate. Cover the grill. Regulate the heat so it remains at a medium temperature. Grill the wings until the skin turns a deep mahogany color, about 30 minutes. Every 5 minutes throughout the grilling process, open the lid, brush the wings with more marinade, turn the wings over, brush again with marinade, then close the lid. Chicken wings are highly sensitive to heat. Keep those wings moving!

With the lid closed, keep the heat in the 300 to 350°F range.

To add a more intense smoky flavor, add hardwood chips, oak bark, or barrel staves. This is an especially useful technique for gas grills because the gas flames and their vaporizing slats or lava rocks do not contribute the concentrated flavor that wings acquire when cooked over briquettes, lump hardwood charcoal, and wood. Wood chips are available at supermarkets and hardware stores. Soak approximately 1 cup of wood chips in cold water for 30 minutes, then drain. Scatter the chips over the charcoal just before adding the wings. On gas grills, place the chips on a layer of aluminum foil positioned on the cooking grate at the corner of the grill. Wait until the wood begins to smoke, place the wings in the rib rack, and cover with the top.

SMOKING

Slow-smoking, what most Southerners call "barbecuing," means cooking wings in a closed, smoke-filled container where the heat is maintained at an even 200 to 220°F (often called "hot smoking"). During the long time required to cook through, the wings acquire a deep smoky flavor and become marvelously tender.

There are hundreds of manufacturers of smokers, most of which are located in the South. Inexpensive electric smokers are sold at most home discount centers nationwide and at all stores specializing in barbecue equipment. In case you are thinking about using your gas grill, don't! Gas grills can't maintain the low constant temperature required for slow smoking.

For smoking, it's always better to err on the side of heat that's too low. Light around 14 briquettes or lump hardwood charcoal to provide the heat for every 1 hour of smoking. Add 14 more lighted briquettes once an hour. Insert an instant-read thermometer into one of the vents in the lid so you can always tell the temperature of the smoker.

QUICK SMOKING DIRECTIONS

Marinate and then smoke the wings "open" (see page 3, figure A) for even cooking. We like to leave the wing tips attached. They're the handles! Preheat an electric smoker, or build a small charcoal fire in a kettle-style or a similar charcoal grill, bringing the temperature to 200 to 220°F. Transfer the wings to the smoker and cook for about 2 hours. The wings are done when the skin turns a deep mahogany color. After 1 hour, brush the wings with a marinade, turn the wings over, and brush with more marinade. After another 30 minutes, baste and turn the wings again.

Charcoal creates the heat, and hardwood chips create the smoky flavor. You can use one wood or a blend of woods when smoking.

Because using large amounts of wood can give the wings an overwhelming smoky, acrid flavor, it is better to err on the side of using too little wood. Add just enough to maintain a smoky atmosphere. To avoid extinguishing the fire, shake excess water off wood chunks before placing them on top of the hot charcoal.

Lift the lid as little as possible, about every 15 minutes. Every time the lid is lifted, 15 minutes of cooking time should be added. The greater the amount of wings in the smoker, the longer they will take to cook.

Keep cooking notes so that you can use the notes as a guide the next time you smoke wings. Experiment!

WOOD CHIPS AND CHUNKS

Alder: light, delicate flavor
Apple and cherry: sweet, fruity flavor
Hickory: strong hickory flavor
Maple: sweet flavor
Mesquite: pungent; will give food a bitter flavor with too much smoking
Oak: assertive flavor and most versatile
Pecan: subtle, rich flavor

OVEN-ROASTING

Tender Meat, Crispy Skin

Oven-roasted chicken wings are The Best! The heat is even and is easily controllable. And the intensely pleasing smell drifts through the house to create the perfect welcoming note when guests arrive.

Use a heavy baking sheet with shallow sides. Line the baking sheet with heavy-duty aluminum foil, and then position a nonstick wire rack on top. Even though wire racks claim to be "nonstick," spray them liberally on both sides with a nonstick oil or rub them with a vegetable oil.

Lay the marinated chicken wings smooth skin side down. This is the pretty side! The wings are turned halfway through the cooking process so that the pretty side colors evenly.

Preheat the oven to 375°F. If your oven has a convection setting, set the oven on convection at 350°F.

Slide the pan holding the wings onto an oven rack positioned in the middle of the oven.

Baste and turn the wings midway (about 30 minutes) through the cooking time. Don't baste them

QUICK OVEN-ROASTING DIRECTIONS

Marinate, then roast the wings "open" (see page 3, figure A) for even cooking. We like to cut off and discard the wing tips—or save them for stock—because the wings get crowded on the wire rack. Place the wings on a wire rack, smooth skin side down (see photo on page 14). Roast in a preheated 375°F oven (convection roast at 350°F if your oven has that setting), and cook for 30 minutes. Brush the wings with the marinade, turn the wings over, and brush again with the marinade. Roast the chicken wings another 30 minutes. It's during the final 30 minutes of cooking that the wings turn an amazing mahogany color.

again or the skin will never acquire the amazing, even mahogany color.

When you turn the wings over, if any moisture has accumulated on the bottom of the baking pan, pour this off and discard. If you don't, then the wings will steam during the final 30 minutes of roasting and the skin will never color properly.

Remove the wings from the oven. Wait 5 minutes before cutting each wing in half.

BRAISING

Braising is a great technique for wings. After a few simple preparation steps, braising sets the cook free to pursue other activities, culinary or not!

Choose a heavy 12- or 14-inch pan with 3-inch sides and a tight-fitting top.

Always cut off and discard the wing tips, and then cut the wings in half through the joint. It's important that the wings snuggle closely together so that they are all equally covered with the braising liquid.

Preheat the pan until it becomes hot. Once the pan is hot, add the braising liquid. There should be enough liquid to cover all the wings so that they cook evenly. Add the wings and bring the sauce to a simmer.

Keep the pan tightly covered. Regulate the heat so that the liquid is at a simmer with only a few bubbles rising to the surface, and never at a boil. If wings boil, the meat will become dry and flavorless.

QUICK BRAISING DIRECTIONS

Cut off and discard the wing tips, then cut the wings in half through the joint. Place a heavy stew pot over medium heat. Add the sauce and bring to a boil. Add the wings. Bring the sauce to a low simmer. Cover the pot, and reduce the heat to low so that the sauce is at a simmer with only a few bubbles rising to the surface. Cook until the meat becomes tender, about 30 minutes of gentle cooking. After about 15 minutes, stir the wings. When the wings are cooked through, temporarily remove them from the liquid. Using strips of paper towels, lift off all the oil that is floating on the surface of the sauce. Return the wings to the sauce. Their skin will be soft, not crispy.

The wings are done when the meat tastes tender, about 30 minutes total cooking time. Taste, and taste, and taste!

Before serving, it's important to remove all fat floating on the surface of the sauce. Otherwise, the sauce tastes greasy. Once the wings become tender, temporarily remove the wings, and then using strips of paper toweling, skim the fat off the surface. Or allow the liquid to cool completely, refrigerate, and spoon the hardened fat off the top.

Return the wings to the sauce and serve. Or if you want a more intense flavor, return the wings to the sauce and turn the heat to medium. Cook the wings, stirring occasionally, until the sauce reduces and forms a thick glaze around the wings.

Wings can be left for up to 1 hour at room temperature and then gently reheated. If cooked further ahead than 1 hour, refrigerate the wings. Braised wings also taste delicious reheated the following day.

DEEP-FRYING

Deep-frying creates a crisp skin while keeping the meat succulent. This wonderful technique, though, does require calm nerves, a steady hand, and practice. Try these recipes out on your family first, several times, before serving these to dinner guests.

Cut off and discard the wing tips. Then cut the wings in half through the joint. Individual pieces are easier to move around in the oil.

Wings are always coated with a protective layer such as white flour, powdered breadcrumbs, or batter to prevent the oil from splattering. To make the coating stick evenly to the chicken wings, make sure the wings are completely free of moisture by drying

QUICK DEEP-FRYING DIRECTIONS

Cut the tips off the wings, and cut the wings in half through the joint. Place a heavy 12- to 14-inch frying pan over medium-high heat. Add 1 inch of flavorless cooking oil. Heat the oil until bubbles form around the end of a wooden spoon dipped into the oil, or until it reaches 350 to 360°F on a deep-frying thermometer. Meanwhile, dust the wings with white flour or powdered breadcrumbs, or dip the wings into a batter. Turn the heat to high and add a single layer of wings. You may need to cook these in several batches. Using long-handled tongs, cook the wings until golden on the underside, about 3 minutes, and then turn the wings over. Cook the wings until they are golden on both sides. Continue cooking until the wings are crisp and fully cooked—about 10 minutes total cooking time. The oil should bubble continuously around the edges of the wings but never be so hot that it smokes. Cut into a wing to make sure it is done. Drain on a wire rack that is placed on a shallow baking pan lined with paper towels. Repeat the cooking process with the remaining wings. Serve at once.

them thoroughly with a paper towel or allowing them to air-dry for up to an hour.

A good heat source and plenty of ventilation are necessities. An easy answer is to use an outdoor gas barbecue. A gas grill turned to high will keep the oil bubbling around the wings, and only the birds flying overhead will be aware of the oil smell. Don't use a charcoal grill. It will ruin the underside of the pan.

Choose a heavy pan that holds heat well. Cast-iron frying pans work best.

Set up your workstation. For a right-handed person, the uncooked wings and batter are positioned on the right side of the frying pan and the wire rack for draining the wings is on the left. Have ready long-handled tongs and oven mitts.

Choose a high-heat flavorless cooking oil such as peanut oil, safflower oil, grapeseed oil, corn oil, or canola oil. Never use olive oil or sesame oil, which smoke at a low temperature.

How much oil should go into the frying pan? A 1-inch depth is perfect. Although the wings will only be half submerged, you'll be turning them several times. Your indoor stovetop or outdoor gas grill will not generate high enough heat to maintain a larger quantity of oil in the essential 350 to 375°F temperature range.

As with all deep-frying, the key is to maintain the oil temperature in the 350 to 375°F temperature range. As long as the oil is continuously bubbling around the chicken wing pieces but is not so hot that it smokes, the oil is in the correct temperature range.

Always err on cooking too few pieces at a time, rather than too many. An overloaded frying pan will cause the oil temperature to plummet below 350°F. Then no matter how hot the oil temperature later becomes, the chicken wings will taste greasy.

The wings will take between 10 and 15 minutes to cook through. Just because the batter has turned a crisp golden isn't a fail-safe indicator that the wings are fully cooked. Cut into a wing with a paring knife. The meat should be cooked right to the bone.

Always serve deep-fried wings immediately. Once these wings cool to room temperature, the batter will no longer taste crisp. And there is no reheating method that can recrisp the exterior.

GREAT
ALL-AMERICAN
WINGS
A National Passion

Throughout this book, recipes refer to "your favorite hot sauce." This is any chile-based sauce such as Tabasco, Chinese Chili Garlic Sauce, or Thai Sweet Red Chili Sauce, and should not be confused with the very mild tomato-based chili sauces made by companies such as Heinz.

CLASSIC BUFFALO WINGS

Serves 4 as an entrée or 6 to 12 as an appetizer

BLUE CHEESE DRESSING

1 cup crumbled blue cheese

½ cup buttermilk

½ cup mayonnaise

2 to 4 tablespoons whipping cream, half-and-half, or milk

2 teaspoons Worcestershire sauce

½ teaspoon salt

¼ teaspoon freshly ground black pepper

24 chicken wings

1 teaspoon salt

1 teaspoon freshly ground black pepper

1 to 3 tablespoons hot sauce

4 tablespoons unsalted butter

1 tablespoon vinegar, any kind

4 cups flavorless cooking oil

Carrot sticks and/or celery sticks, for serving

To make the dressing, in an electric blender, place ½ cup of the blue cheese and all the remaining ingredients and liquefy. For a thinner consistency, add a little more whipping cream. Stir in the remaining ½ cup blue cheese. This can be done up to 12 hours before cooking, and then stored, tightly covered, in the refrigerator.

Cut off and discard the chicken wing tips. Cut the wings in half through the joint. You will have 48 pieces. Rub the chicken with salt and pepper. Place the hot sauce, butter, and vinegar in a small saucepan. Bring the mixture to a simmer, then set aside.

Place a 12-inch frying pan over medium-high heat on an indoor stovetop or an outdoor gas grill. Add the cooking oil. Heat the oil until bubbles form around the end of a wooden spoon dipped into the oil, 350 to 375°F. Turn the heat to high. Add half the chicken wings. Deep-fry until the wings become deep golden and the meat is cooked along the bone (cut into one with a paring knife), about 12 minutes. Transfer the wings to a wire rack to drain. Cook the second batch of wings. Place the wings on a serving platter. Pour the butter sauce over the wings. Serve with the dressing and the carrot sticks.

CHILI-COATED BUFFALO WINGS

Serves 4 as the entrée or 6 to 12 as an appetizer

24 chicken wings
2 teaspoons salt
2 teaspoons chili powder
1 teaspoon paprika
1 teaspoon cayenne powder
1 teaspoon ground coriander
1 teaspoon freshly ground black pepper
1 teaspoon garlic powder
2 cups unbleached white flour
4 cups flavorless cooking oil
¼ cup your favorite hot sauce or Tabasco sauce
1 recipe Blue Cheese Dressing (page 23)
Carrot sticks and/or celery sticks, for serving

Cut off the wing tips and save them for making stock. Cut the wings in half through the joint. In a bowl, combine the salt, chili powder, paprika, cayenne, coriander, pepper, and garlic powder. Stir to mix evenly. Rub the wings with the mixture, then refrigerate for 1 to 8 hours.

Rub the wings with the flour. Place a 12-inch frying pan over medium-high heat on an indoor stovetop or an outdoor gas grill. Add the cooking oil. Heat the oil until bubbles form around the end of a wooden spoon dipped into the oil (350 to 375°F). Turn the heat to high. Add half the wings. Cook until a deep golden and the meat is cooked along the bone (cut into one with a paring knife). Total cooking time is about 12 minutes. Transfer the wings to a wire rack to drain. Cook the second batch of wings. Transfer the wings to a serving platter. Pour the hot sauce over the wings. Serve with the dressing and the carrot sticks.

BRAISED SOUTHWEST WINGS

Serves 4 as an entrée or 6 to 12 as an appetizer

24 chicken wings
2 cups store-bought barbecue sauce
1 cup honey
1 cup wine vinegar
2 tablespoons American chili powder
2 teaspoons ground cumin
4 cloves garlic, minced
4 jalapeño or serrano chiles, minced, including the seeds

Cut off the wing tips and save them for making stock. Cut the wings in half through the joint. In a bowl, combine all the remaining ingredients. Place a deep 12-inch pan over medium-low heat. When hot, add the sauce. Bring to a simmer. Stir in the wings. Bring the liquid to a low boil, cover, turn the heat to low, and simmer, stirring occasionally, until the chicken wings become very tender, about 30 minutes. These can be made up to a day before serving.

Right before serving, bring the wings to a low boil.

Most of the "heat" in fresh chiles comes from the ribbing and seeds. Rather than cutting the chile in half and struggling to remove the seeds and ribbing, mince the entire chile (seeds and ribbing, too!), but use fewer chiles. This speeds up the preparation.

CAJUN BUFFALO WINGS

Serves 4 as an entrée or 6 to 12 as an appetizer

24 chicken wings
1 cup mild tomato chili sauce (we like Heinz Premium Chili Sauce)
¾ cup honey
1 cup red wine vinegar
¼ cup Worcestershire sauce
1 tablespoon crushed red chile flakes
6 cloves garlic, minced
¼ cup chopped fresh oregano
1 green onion, ends trimmed, minced

Cut off wing tips and save them for making stock. In a bowl large enough to hold the wings, combine all the remaining ingredients. Add the wings and mix thoroughly. Marinate the wings in the refrigerator for 1 to 24 hours (the longer, the better).

Preheat the oven to 375°F. Line a shallow baking pan with foil. Coat a wire rack with nonstick cooking spray and place the rack in the baking pan. Drain the chicken and reserve the marinade. Arrange the wings on the rack (smooth surface down) and roast for 30 minutes. Drain the accumulated liquid from the pan. Baste the wings with the reserved marinade, turn them over, and baste again. Roast until the wings turn a mahogany color, about another 30 minutes. Cut the wings in half through the joint. Serve hot or at room temperature.

WINGS WITH LEMON GLAZE

Serves 4 as an entrée or 6 to 12 as an appetizer

24 chicken wings

LEMON GLAZE
1½ cups freshly squeezed lemon juice
1 cup sugar
¾ cup chicken broth
6 tablespoons thin soy sauce
½ teaspoon salt
1 tablespoon cornstarch

Cut off the wing tips and save them for making stock.

To make the glaze, in a small saucepan, combine all the glaze ingredients and bring to a simmer. Cool to room temperature. Pour over the wings and turn to coat evenly.

Preheat the oven to 375°F. Line a shallow baking pan with foil. Coat a wire rack with nonstick cooking spray and place the rack in the baking pan. Drain the wings and reserve the glaze. Arrange the wings on the rack (smooth surface down) and roast for 30 minutes. Drain the accumulated liquid from the pan. Brush the wings with the glaze, turn the wings over, and baste again. Roast until the wings turn a mahogany color, about another 30 minutes. Cut the wings in half through the joint. Serve hot or at room temperature.

This lemon mop is great brushed across chicken wings just before they are pulled out of the oven or off the barbecue grill. The lemon glaze adds a great extra flavor, no matter what style of marinade or dry rub coats the wings. The Lemon Glaze is also excellent used as a dipping sauce for lollipop wings; add 2 teaspoons cornstarch to the lemon mixture, then bring it to a boil so that it thickens slightly. Use hot or at room temperature.

What's more American than peanut butter and jelly and chicken wings! The rich-tasting peanut butter causes the marinade to thicken around the wings. The jelly (any kind) adds sweetness that is nicely balanced by the sourness of orange juice, and the chile sauce adds that lingering heat. People keep coming back for more.

PEANUT BUTTER AND JELLY WINGS

Serves 4 as an entrée or 6 to 12 as an appetizer

24 chicken wings
½ cup peanut butter
1 cup jelly (raspberry, strawberry, blackberry)
1 cup wine vinegar
1 cup freshly squeezed orange juice
2 tablespoons your favorite hot sauce
4 cloves garlic, minced

Cut off the wing tips and save them for making stock. In a bowl large enough to hold the wings, combine all the remaining ingredients. Add the wings and mix thoroughly. Marinate the wings in the refrigerator for 1 to 24 hours (the longer, the better).

Preheat the oven to 375°F. Line a shallow baking pan with foil. Coat a wire rack with nonstick cooking spray and place the rack in the baking pan. Drain the chicken and reserve the marinade. Arrange the wings on the rack (smooth surface down) and roast for 30 minutes. Drain the accumulated liquid from the pan. Baste the wings with the reserved marinade, turn them over, and baste again. Roast until the wings turn a mahogany color, about another 30 minutes. Cut the wings in half through the joint. Serve hot or at room temperature.

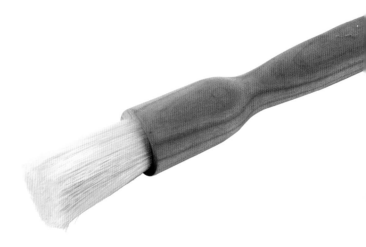

BEST EVER AMERICAN WINGS

Serves 4 as an entrée or 6 to 12 as an appetizer

24 chicken wings
4 cups red wine
3 cups ketchup
½ cup Heinz 57 Sauce
6 tablespoons brown sugar
¼ cup chili powder
2 tablespoons molasses
1 tablespoon dried oregano
1 tablespoon dried thyme
1 tablespoon paprika
1 tablespoon Tabasco sauce
3 tablespoons flavorless cooking oil
6 cloves garlic, minced

Cut off the wing tips and save them for making stock. In a large bowl, combine the red wine, ketchup, Heinz 57, brown sugar, chili powder, molasses, oregano, thyme, paprika, and Tabasco sauce. In a 12-inch sauté pan, add the oil and sauté the garlic. When the garlic begins to brown, add the red wine mixture. Bring to a low boil, then simmer for 20 minutes. Cool to room temperature. In a bowl large enough to hold the wings, combine the wings and the red wine sauce. Mix thoroughly. Marinate the wings in the refrigerator for 1 to 24 hours (the longer, the better).

Preheat the oven to 375°F. Line a shallow baking pan with foil. Coat a wire rack with nonstick cooking spray and place the rack in the baking pan. Drain the chicken and reserve the marinade. Arrange the wings on the rack (smooth surface down) and roast for 30 minutes. Drain the accumulated liquid from the pan. Baste the wings with the reserved marinade, turn them over, and baste again. Roast until the wings turn a mahogany color, about another 30 minutes. Cut the wings in half through the joint. Serve hot or at room temperature.

CAROLINA BBQ WINGS

Serves 4 as an entrée or 6 to 12 as an appetizer

24 chicken wings
¼ cup chili powder
1 tablespoon freshly ground black pepper
1 tablespoon brown sugar

CAROLINA BBQ SAUCE
3 tablespoons flavorless cooking oil
1 medium yellow onion, chopped
4 cloves garlic, minced
1 cup brown sugar
2 cups ketchup
¾ cup vinegar, any kind
¼ cup Worcestershire sauce
¼ cup your favorite hot sauce
2 green onions, ends trimmed, minced
1 teaspoon salt

Cut off the wing tips and save them for making stock. In a bowl large enough to hold the wings, combine the chili powder, pepper, and sugar. Add the wings, and mix thoroughly, rubbing the spices into the skin. Marinate the wings in the refrigerator for 1 to 24 hours (the longer, the better).

To make the sauce, place a 12-inch sauté pan over medium heat. Add the oil. Add the onion. When the onion browns, about 6 minutes, add the garlic. After 30 seconds add all the remaining sauce ingredients. Bring to a low boil, then reduce the heat to low and simmer for 15 minutes. Let cool and refrigerate if made more than 2 hours before using.

Combine the wings with the sauce. If using a gas barbecue or an indoor grill, preheat to medium (350°F). If using charcoal or wood, prepare a fire. Drain the chicken and reserve the sauce. When the barbecue is preheated, brush the grill with oil, then add the wings. Regulate the heat at a medium temperature. Grill the wings for about 30 minutes with the barbecue covered. Turn the wings every 5 minutes, basting them on both sides with the sauce until the skin turns an even mahogany color and the meat is tender.

Remove the wings from the barbecue. Cut each in half through the joint to separate "drumstick" from wing. Serve.

Caramelizing the onion gives barbecue sauce an extra depth of flavor. It's important to do this over low heat, or the natural sugars on the surface of the onion will burn. It takes about 15 minutes to complete this process, during which time the rest of the barbecue sauce ingredients can be measured.

For an intense citrus taste, use grated lime zest and freshly squeezed lime juice. Use a microplane (see opposite page) to quickly grate the colored skin of the lime. This is vastly quicker than struggling with a cheese grater. As for store-bought lime juice, both the refrigerated type and the little green lime-shaped "grenades" are taste travesties.

BBQ SPICY CITRUS WINGS

Serves 4 as an entrée or 6 to 12 as an appetizer

24 chicken wings
1 cup Heinz 57 Sauce
2 tablespoons grated lime zest
1 cup freshly squeezed lime juice
½ cup firmly packed light brown sugar
½ cup thin soy sauce
¼ cup your favorite hot sauce
4 cloves garlic, minced

Cut off the wing tips and save them for making stock. In a bowl large enough to hold the wings, combine all the remaining ingredients. Add the wings and mix thoroughly. Marinate the wings in the refrigerator for 1 to 24 hours (the longer, the better).

If using a gas barbecue or an indoor grill, preheat to medium (350°F). If using charcoal or wood, prepare a fire. Drain the chicken and reserve the sauce. When the gas barbecue or indoor grill is preheated or the coals or wood are ash covered, brush the grill with oil, then add the chicken wings. Regulate the heat so that it remains at a medium temperature. Grill the chicken wings for about 30 minutes with the barbecue covered. Turn the wings every 5 minutes, basting them on both sides with the sauce. The chicken wings are done when the skin turns an even mahogany color and the meat is tender.

Remove the chicken wings from the barbecue. Cut the wings in half through the joint. Transfer to a serving platter and serve.

BRAISED WINGS TEXAS STYLE

Serves 4 as an entrée or 6 to 12 as an appetizer

24 chicken wings

2 tablespoons freshly ground black pepper

1 tablespoon chili powder

2 tablespoons ground coriander

2 tablespoons ground cumin

1 teaspoon salt

2 teaspoons ground cinnamon

8 cloves garlic, minced

2 cups chopped vine-ripened tomatoes, including seeds and skin
(fresh or boxed store-bought chopped tomatoes)

2 cups dry red wine

¼ cup firmly packed brown sugar

2 teaspoons crushed red chile flakes

3 tablespoons chopped cilantro sprigs

Cut off the wing tips and save them for making stock. Cut the wings in half through the joint. In a large bowl, combine the pepper, chili powder, coriander, cumin, salt, cinnamon, and garlic. Rub this evenly over all the chicken wings. In another bowl, combine the tomatoes, wine, brown sugar, chile flakes, and cilantro.

Heat a heavy pan to medium-hot. Add the tomato mixture and bring to a simmer. Add the wings and bring to a simmer. Cover the pan and lower the heat. Simmer until the wings become tender, about 30 minutes. Stir occasionally. Cook until nearly all the sauce evaporates and forms a glaze around the wings. Serve.

BRAISED WINGS
WITH LEMON AND CHILES

Serves 4 as an entrée or 6 to 12 as an appetizer

24 chicken wings
3 tablespoons flavorless cooking oil
2 cloves garlic, minced
2 tablespoons minced ginger
2 tablespoons grated lemon zest
1 cup freshly squeezed lemon juice
1 cup chicken broth
6 tablespoons sugar
2 tablespoons thin soy sauce
2 teaspoons Asian chile sauce or your favorite hot sauce
½ teaspoon salt

Cut off the wing tips and save them for making stock. Cut the wings in half through the joint. Place a deep 12-inch pan over medium-low heat. Add the oil and the chicken wings. Cook until the wings brown, about 6 minutes. Add the garlic and ginger and cook 1 minute more.

Meanwhile, combine all the remaining ingredients in a bowl and pour over the wings. Bring the liquid to a low boil, cover, turn the heat to low, and simmer until the chicken wings become very tender, about 30 minutes. Stir occasionally. Once the chicken is cooked through, bring to a low boil and continue cooking until nearly all the sauce evaporates and forms a glaze around the wings. The wings can be made up to 1 day in advance, reheated, and served.

A common New Orleans flavor profile includes spicy sausage, Worcestershire sauce, fresh oregano, garlic, and cream. I've tried this recipe with the smoked andouille sausage, typical of New Orleans cooking, and compared it with using spicy sausage meat available at every market. Both are excellent. If you use andouille sausage, finely mince it, either with a knife or in a food processor.

NEW ORLEANS—INSPIRED WINGS

Serves 4 as an entrée and 6 to 12 as an appetizer

24 chicken wings

3 tablespoons extra-virgin olive oil

½ pound spicy sausage meat

1 yellow onion, chopped

6 cloves garlic, minced

2 tablespoons chopped fresh oregano leaves

2 cups chopped vine-ripened tomatoes, including seeds and skin
(fresh or boxed store-bought chopped tomatoes)

1 cup heavy cream

2 tablespoons Worcestershire sauce

1 tablespoon your favorite hot sauce

½ teaspoon salt

⅓ cup chopped parsley

Cut off the wing tips and save them for making stock. Cut the wings in half through the joint. Place a deep 12-inch pan over medium heat. Add the olive oil. When hot, add the sausage and onion. Cook until the onion browns, about 12 minutes, stirring occasionally. Meanwhile, in a large bowl, combine the garlic, oregano, tomatoes, heavy cream, Worcestershire sauce, hot sauce, and salt. Add the wings and the tomato sauce to the onions. Bring to a low boil. Cover, turn the heat to low, and simmer until the chicken wings become very tender, about 30 minutes. Stir occasionally. This can be done 24 hours prior to serving.

To serve, bring the wings and sauce to a low boil. Cook until nearly all the sauce evaporates and forms a glaze around the wings. Stir in the parsley just before serving.

WAY-DOWN-SOUTH WINGS

Serves 4 as an entrée or 6 to 12 as an appetizer

24 chicken wings

3 tablespoons olive oil

2 shallots, minced

6 cloves garlic, minced

2 tablespoons chopped fresh oregano

2 tablespoons minced tender thyme ends

2 cups chicken broth

1½ cups ketchup

¼ cup Worcestershire sauce

3 tablespoons brown sugar

2 tablespoons molasses

1 tablespoon Tabasco sauce

2 tablespoons chili powder

Cut off the wing tips and save them for making stock. Cut the wings in half through the joint. Place a deep 12-inch pan over medium heat. Add the olive oil. When hot, add the wings. Brown the wings on all sides, about 6 minutes. Add the shallots and garlic, and cook 1 minute more. Meanwhile, in a large bowl, combine all the remaining ingredients. After the garlic has been cooked for 1 minute, add the sauce. Bring to a boil. Cover, turn the heat to low, and simmer until the chicken wings become very tender, about 30 minutes. Stir occasionally. This can be done 24 hours prior to serving.

To serve, bring the wings and sauce to a low boil. Cook until nearly all the sauce evaporates and forms a glaze around the wings. Serve.

AMERICAN STUFFED WINGS

Serves 4 as an entrée or 6 to 12 as an appetizer

24 chicken wings

1 ear corn

2 green onions, ends trimmed, minced

1 pound ground lamb

2 cloves garlic, minced

1 tablespoon Worcestershire sauce

½ cup ketchup

½ teaspoon salt

2 cups your favorite barbecue sauce
(we like Red Tail Ale BBQ Sauce)

¼ cup chopped parsley

Prepare the chicken wings for stuffing (see page 7). Cut the kernels off the corn. In a bowl, combine the corn kernels, green onions, lamb, garlic, Worcestershire sauce, ketchup, and salt. Using your fingers, mix until evenly blended. Transfer the stuffing to a pastry bag and fill the wings. This can be done up to 12 hours in advance of cooking; keep refrigerated.

Preheat the oven to 375°F. Line a shallow baking pan with foil. Coat a wire rack with nonstick cooking spray and place the rack in the baking pan. Coat the wings with the barbecue sauce. Place the wings in a single layer on the rack. Place the baking pan in the middle of the oven and roast for 45 minutes. Sprinkle with the chopped parsley. Serve hot.

Make the Apricot Mop one of your standard "go-to" condiments. It lasts indefinitely in the refrigerator and is great brushed on any meat or seafood coming off the barbecue grill. You can also use it as a dipping sauce for chilled jumbo shrimp, or add it to salad dressing for an apricot vinaigrette. And if you omit the chile sauce, the Apricot Mop is great on pancakes, waffles, cheesecakes, and ice cream.

CRISPY LOLLIPOPS WITH APRICOT MOP

Serves 4 as an entrée and 6 to 12 as an appetizer

12 chicken wings
2 cups buttermilk
½ cup chopped cilantro sprigs
6 cloves garlic, minced
1 tablespoon crushed red chile flakes
1 tablespoon salt
1¼ cups unbleached white flour
2 cups flavorless cooking oil

APRICOT MOP
2 cups apricot jam
1 cup white distilled vinegar
1 cup water
2 tablespoons minced ginger
2 teaspoons Asian chile sauce

Lollipop the chicken wings (see page 4). In a bowl, combine the buttermilk, cilantro, garlic, chile flakes, salt, and flour. Stir well. Pour the batter into a 9 × 9-inch baking pan. Add the chicken wings, meaty side down, so the meaty ends are completely coated with the batter. Marinate the wings in the refrigerator for 1 to 24 hours (the longer, the better).

To make the mop, in a saucepan, combine all the mop ingredients. Bring to a low boil, then cool to room temperature. This can be done 24 hours before cooking; place everything in the refrigerator.

To cook, warm the mop in a saucepan. Place a 12-inch frying pan over medium-high heat on an indoor stovetop or an outdoor gas grill. Add the cooking oil. Heat the oil until bubbles form around the end of a wooden spoon dipped into the oil (350 to 375°F). Place 12 lollipops meaty side down into the oil. Deep-fry until the batter becomes deep golden and the meat is cooked along the bone (cut into one with a paring knife). Total cooking time is about 8 minutes. Transfer the wings to a wire rack to drain. Cook the second batch of wings. Serve with the Apricot Mop or your favorite dipping sauce.

SPICY LOLLIPOP WINGS

Serves 4 as an entrée or 6 to 12 as an appetizer

12 chicken wings
4 cloves garlic, minced
1 teaspoon ground cumin
1 teaspoon ground coriander
1 teaspoon ground cinnamon
1 teaspoon salt
1 teaspoon crushed red chile flakes
¼ cup chopped parsley

THE MOP
1 tablespoon grated lime zest
½ cup freshly squeezed lime juice
½ cup sugar
½ cup water
1 tablespoon cornstarch
½ teaspoon salt
½ teaspoon crushed red chile flakes

Lollipop the chicken wings (see page 4). You should have 24 pieces. Using your fingers, rub the garlic into the lollipop chicken wing meat. In a bowl, combine the cumin, coriander, cinnamon, salt, and chile flakes. Stir to mix evenly, then rub the spices into the meat. This can be done 12 hours before cooking; keep refrigerated.

To make the mop, in a small saucepan, combine the mop ingredients. Place over medium heat. Stir until the mop boils. Set aside.

Preheat the oven to 375°F. Line a shallow baking pan with foil. Coat a wire rack with nonstick cooking spray and place the rack in the baking pan. Dip each lollipop into the sauce. Stand the lollipops, meaty end downward, on the wire rack. Place in the oven and roast for 30 minutes. Brush the meat with the mop after 15 minutes of cooking. When the wings are cooked, transfer to a serving platter. Sprinkle with the parsley. Serve at once.

GREAT
LATIN AND EUROPEAN
WINGS
A New Vision for Wings

BRAISED WINGS WITH RED WINE AND MUSHROOM SAUCE

Serves 4 as an entrée or 6 to 12 as an appetizer

24 chicken wings

3 tablespoons unsalted butter

2 small yellow onions, chopped

4 cloves garlic, minced

4 cups chopped brown button mushrooms

2 cups red wine

2 cups chicken broth

4 teaspoons tomato paste

1 teaspoon sugar

2 tablespoons chopped fresh thyme
or oregano leaves

2 teaspoons crushed red chile flakes

1 teaspoon salt

Cut off the wing tips and save them for making stock. Cut the wings in half through the joint. Place a deep 12-inch pan over medium-low heat. Add the butter and the onions. Cook until the onion browns, about 12 minutes. Add the garlic and mushrooms to the pan. Cook until the mushrooms wilt, about 6 minutes. Meanwhile, in a large bowl, combine all the remaining ingredients. Pour into the pan and bring to a low boil. Add the wings. Bring the liquid to a low boil, cover, turn the heat to low, and simmer until the chicken wings become very tender, about 30 minutes. Stir occasionally. This can be done 24 hours prior to serving.

To serve, bring the wings and sauce to a low boil. Cook until nearly all the sauce evaporates and forms a glaze around the wings. Serve. Can be reheated and served the next day.

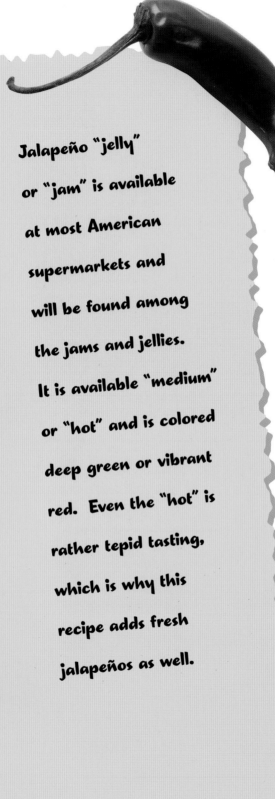

Jalapeño "jelly" or "jam" is available at most American supermarkets and will be found among the jams and jellies. It is available "medium" or "hot" and is colored deep green or vibrant red. Even the "hot" is rather tepid tasting, which is why this recipe adds fresh jalapeños as well.

MEXICAN WINGS WITH JALAPEÑO GLAZE

Serves 4 as an entrée or 6 to 12 as an appetizer

24 chicken wings
1 teaspoon salt
2 teaspoons freshly ground black pepper
1 tablespoon ground cumin
4 cloves garlic, minced
2 cups jalapeño jam
2 cups freshly squeezed orange juice
2 jalapeño chiles, minced, including the seeds
¼ cup chopped cilantro sprigs

Cut off the wing tips and save them for making stock. In a small saucepan, combine all the remaining ingredients. Bring to a simmer, stirring to combine. Let cool to room temperature. In a bowl large enough to hold the wings, combine the wings and the jam mixture. Marinate the wings in the refrigerator for 1 to 24 hours (the longer, the better).

Preheat the oven to 375°F. Line a shallow baking pan with foil. Coat a wire rack with nonstick cooking spray and place the rack in the baking pan. Drain the chicken and reserve the marinade. Arrange the wings on the rack (smooth surface down) and roast for 30 minutes. Drain the accumulated liquid from the pan. Baste the wings with the reserved marinade, turn them over, and baste again. Roast until the wings turn a mahogany color, about another 30 minutes. Cut the wings in half through the joint. Serve hot or at room temperature.

SIZZLING WINGS WITH DIJON MUSTARD RUB

Serves 4 as an entrée or 6 to 12 as an appetizer

24 chicken wings
½ cup chopped parsley
6 cloves garlic, minced
2 shallots, minced
2 tablespoons grated lemon zest
⅔ cup freshly squeezed lemon juice
⅔ cup extra-virgin olive oil
⅔ cup Dijon mustard
⅔ cup thin soy sauce

Cut off the wing tips and save them for making stock. In a bowl large enough to hold the wings, combine all the remaining ingredients. Add the wings, and mix thoroughly. Marinate the wings in the refrigerator for 1 to 24 hours (the longer, the better).

Preheat the oven to 375°F. Line a shallow baking pan with foil. Coat a wire rack with nonstick cooking spray and place the rack in the baking pan. Drain the chicken and reserve the marinade. Arrange the wings on the rack (smooth surface down) and roast for 30 minutes. Drain the accumulated liquid from the pan. Baste the wings with the reserved marinade, turn them over, and baste again. Roast until the wings turn a mahogany color, about another 30 minutes. Cut the wings in half through the joint. Serve hot or at room temperature.

MIDDLE EASTERN WINGS

Serves 4 as an entrée or 6 to 12 as an appetizer

24 chicken wings
Grated zest from 2 lemons
1 cup freshly squeezed lemon juice
1 cup extra-virgin olive oil
½ cup honey
1 tablespoon ground cumin
1 tablespoon sweet paprika
2 teaspoons cayenne pepper
1½ teaspoons salt
6 cloves garlic, minced
⅓ cup minced ginger
½ cup chopped cilantro sprigs
½ cup chopped mint leaves
2 teaspoons freshly grated nutmeg

Cut off the wing tips and save them for making stock. In a bowl large enough to hold the wings, combine all the remaining ingredients. Add the wings, and mix thoroughly. Marinate the wings in the refrigerator for 1 to 24 hours (the longer, the better).

Preheat the oven to 375°F. Line a shallow baking pan with foil. Coat a wire rack with nonstick cooking spray and place the rack in the baking pan. Drain the chicken and reserve the marinade. Arrange the wings on the rack (smooth surface down) and roast for 30 minutes. Drain the accumulated liquid from the pan. Baste the wings with the reserved marinade, turn them over, and baste again. Roast until the wings turn a mahogany color, about another 30 minutes. Cut the wings in half through the joint. Serve hot or at room temperature.

Imported black olives are olives allowed to hang on the branches until they turn black; then they are picked and cured. American canned black olives are made from olives picked green off the trees and then chemically treated to turn them black. This practice dates to the early canning industry developed during the American Civil War. Imported black olives are an immense flavor improvement compared to the canned variety.

ROAST WINGS WITH OLIVES, ROSEMARY, AND PINE NUTS

Serves 4 as an entrée or 6 to 12 as an appetizer

24 chicken wings

2 tablespoons grated lemon zest

1 cup freshly squeezed lemon juice

1 cup imported black olives, pitted and minced

½ cup extra-virgin olive oil

¼ cup honey

¼ cup chopped fresh rosemary

6 cloves garlic, minced

2 teaspoons crushed red chile flakes

½ cup pine nuts, toasted and finely chopped

1 teaspoon salt

Cut off the wing tips and save them for making stock. In a bowl, combine all the remaining ingredients. Add the wings, and mix thoroughly. Marinate the wings in the refrigerator for 1 to 24 hours (the longer, the better).

Preheat the oven to 375°F. Line a shallow baking pan with foil. Coat a wire rack with nonstick cooking spray and place the rack in the baking pan. Drain the chicken and reserve the marinade. Arrange the wings on the rack (smooth surface down) and roast for 30 minutes. Drain the accumulated liquid from the pan. Baste the wings with the reserved marinade, turn them over, and baste again. Roast until the wings turn a mahogany color, about another 30 minutes. Cut the wings in half through the joint. Serve hot or at room temperature.

WINGS WITH CHIPOTLE HONEY GLAZE

Serves 4 as an entrée or 6 to 12 as an appetizer

24 chicken wings
8 cloves garlic, minced
½ cup chopped cilantro sprigs
¼ cup chipotle chiles in adobo sauce, minced
2 cups taco sauce
½ cup honey
½ cup vinegar
1 tablespoon ground cumin
1 teaspoon salt
1 cup sour cream (optional)

Cut off the wing tips and save them for making stock. In a bowl large enough to hold the wings, combine the garlic, cilantro, chipotle chiles and their sauce, taco sauce, honey, vinegar, cumin, and salt. Add the wings, and mix thoroughly. Marinate the wings in the refrigerator for 1 to 24 hours (the longer, the better).

If using a gas barbecue or an indoor grill, preheat to medium (350°F). If using charcoal or wood, prepare a fire. Drain the chicken and reserve the marinade. When the gas barbecue or indoor grill is preheated or the coals or wood are ash covered, brush the grill with oil, then add the chicken wings. Regulate the heat so that it remains at a medium temperature. Grill the chicken wings for about 30 minutes with the barbecue covered. Turn the wings every 5 minutes, basting them on both sides with the reserved marinade. The chicken wings are done when the skin turns an even mahogany color and the meat is tender.

Remove the chicken wings from the barbecue. Cut the wings in half through the joint. Transfer to a serving platter, drizzle the sour cream over the wings, and serve.

LATIN WINGS WITH MANGO-CHILI GLAZE

Serves 4 as an entrée or 6 to 12 as an appetizer

24 chicken wings

3 serrano or jalapeño chiles

¼ cup thinly sliced ginger

5 cloves garlic

3 green onions, ends trimmed

¼ cup minced cilantro sprigs or mint leaves

1 (12-ounce) can mango nectar

Fruit from 2 ripe mangoes (about 2 cups)

¼ cup firmly packed brown sugar

1 teaspoon salt

1 teaspoon allspice

Cut off the wing tips and save them for making stock. In a food processor, mince the chiles, ginger, and garlic. Add the green onions and cilantro, and mince. Add all the remaining ingredients and liquefy. In a large bowl, combine the wings and mango mixture. Mix thoroughly. Marinate the wings in the refrigerator for 1 to 24 hours (the longer, the better).

Preheat the oven to 375°F. Line a shallow baking pan with foil. Coat a wire rack with nonstick cooking spray and place the rack in the baking pan. Drain the chicken and reserve the marinade. Arrange the wings on the rack (smooth surface down) and roast for 30 minutes. Drain the accumulated liquid from the pan. Baste the wings with the reserved marinade, turn them over, and baste again. Roast until the wings turn a mahogany color, about another 30 minutes. Cut the wings in half through the joint. Serve hot or at room temperature.

Mango nectar is sold in the juice section of most supermarkets and is used to add volume to the marinade. But it's the fresh ripe mangoes that contribute the tropical Latin flavor. Make this recipe only when perfectly ripe mangoes are available. They should be slightly soft to the touch. Using a paring knife, remove the skin, and cut away the flesh in large pieces. Then mince or puree.

BBQ WINGS WITH POMEGRANATE GLAZE

Serves 4 as an entrée or 6 to 12 as an appetizer

24 chicken wings

1½ cups pomegranate molasses

3 tablespoons grated lemon zest

¾ cup freshly squeezed lemon juice

2 tablespoons ground coriander

1 tablespoon crushed red chile flakes

⅓ cup minced ginger

4 cloves garlic, minced

2 green onions, ends trimmed, minced

¼ cup chopped rosemary sprigs

Cut off the wing tips and save them for making stock. In a bowl large enough to hold the wings, combine all the remaining ingredients. Add the wings, and mix thoroughly. Marinate the wings in the refrigerator for 1 to 24 hours (the longer, the better).

If using a gas barbecue or an indoor grill, preheat to medium (350°F). If using charcoal or wood, prepare a fire. Drain the chicken and reserve the marinade. When the gas barbecue or indoor grill is preheated or the coals or wood are ash covered, brush the grill with oil, then add the chicken wings. Regulate the heat so that it remains at a medium temperature. Grill the chicken wings for about 30 minutes with the barbecue covered. Turn the wings every 5 minutes, basting them on both sides with the reserved marinade. The chicken wings are done when the skin turns an even mahogany color and the meat is tender.

Remove the chicken wings from the barbecue. Cut the wings in half through the joint. Transfer to a platter and serve.

Habanero chiles are one of this planet's hottest chiles. Ranging in color from light green to bright orange to deep yellow, they are 1 inch in diameter, irregularly shaped, and similar to Scotch bonnets. Habanero chiles are native to the Caribbean, the Yucatan Peninsula, and the north coast of South America. When handling them, always place your hands in plastic bags. Or substitute less spicy jalapeño or serrano chiles, or your favorite hot sauce.

BBQ WINGS WITH HABANERO-STRAWBERRY GLAZE

Serves 4 as an entrée or 6 to 12 as an appetizer

24 chicken wings

1 cup strawberry jam

Grated or minced zest from 4 limes

1 cup freshly squeezed lime juice

½ cup minced ginger

1 teaspoon salt

½ cup chopped fresh mint

2 habanero chiles, minced, including the seeds

Cut off the wing tips and save them for making stock. In a bowl large enough to hold the wings, combine all the remaining ingredients. Add the wings, and mix thoroughly. Marinate the wings in the refrigerator for 1 to 24 hours (the longer, the better).

If using a gas barbecue or an indoor grill, preheat to medium (350°F). If using charcoal or wood, prepare a fire. Drain the chicken and reserve the marinade. When the gas barbecue or indoor grill is preheated or the coals or wood are ash covered, brush the grill with oil, then add the chicken wings. Regulate the heat so that it remains at a medium temperature. Grill the chicken wings for about 30 minutes with the barbecue covered. Turn the wings every 5 minutes, basting them on both sides with the reserved marinade. The chicken wings are done when the skin turns an even mahogany color and the meat is tender.

Remove the chicken wings from the barbecue. Cut the wings in half through the joint. Transfer to a platter and serve.

JAMAICAN BBQ WINGS

Serves 4 as an entrée or 6 to 12 as an appetizer

24 chicken wings
¼ cup thinly sliced ginger
6 cloves garlic, peeled
4 serrano or jalapeño chiles,
or 2 tablespoons hot sauce
½ cup chopped mint leaves
2 cups fresh pineapple chunks
¼ cup thin soy sauce
¼ cup honey
¼ cup freshly squeezed lime juice
1 teaspoon freshly ground black pepper

Cut off the wing tips and save them for making stock. In a food processor, mince the ginger, garlic, and chiles. Add all the remaining ingredients and process into a smooth paste. Transfer to a large bowl. Add the wings, and mix thoroughly. Marinate the wings in the refrigerator for 1 to 24 hours (the longer, the better).

If using a gas barbecue or an indoor grill, preheat to medium (350°F). If using charcoal or wood, prepare a fire. Drain the chicken and reserve the marinade. When the gas barbecue or indoor grill is preheated or the coals or wood are ash covered, brush the grill with oil, then add the chicken wings. Regulate the heat so that it remains at a medium temperature. Grill the chicken wings for about 30 minutes with the barbecue covered. Turn the wings every 5 minutes, basting them on both sides with the reserved marinade. The chicken wings are done when the skin turns an even mahogany color and the meat is tender.

Remove the chicken wings from the barbecue. Cut the wings in half through the joint. Transfer to a serving platter and serve.

BBQ WINGS WITH MUSTARD, TEQUILA, AND JUNIPER BERRIES

Serves 4 as an entrée or 6 to 12 as an appetizer

24 chicken wings

2 cups tequila, vodka, or gin

1 cup Dijon mustard

1 cup freshly squeezed lemon juice

½ cup honey

½ cup thin soy sauce

1 tablespoon crushed juniper berries, or
3 tablespoons minced rosemary

6 cloves garlic, minced

4 serrano chiles, minced, including the seeds,
or 1 tablespoon your favorite hot sauce

⅓ cup chopped cilantro sprigs

Cut off the wing tips and save them for making stock. In a bowl large enough to hold the wings, combine all the remaining ingredients. Add the wings, and mix thoroughly. Marinate the wings in the refrigerator for 1 to 24 hours (the longer, the better).

If using a gas barbecue or an indoor grill, preheat to medium (350°F). If using charcoal or wood, prepare a fire. Drain the chicken and reserve the marinade. When the gas barbecue or indoor grill is preheated or the coals or wood are ash covered, brush the grill with oil, then add the chicken wings. Regulate the heat so that it remains at a medium temperature. Grill the chicken wings for about 30 minutes with the barbecue covered. Turn the wings every 5 minutes, basting them on both sides with the reserved marinade. The chicken wings are done when the skin turns an even mahogany color and the meat is tender.

Remove the chicken wings from the barbecue. Cut the wings in half through the joint. Transfer to a platter and serve.

ITALIAN STUFFED WINGS

Serves 4 as an entrée or 6 to 12 as an appetizer

24 chicken wings
¼ cup pine nuts, toasted
1 pound ground veal
¼ cup chopped roasted red pepper (bottled variety)
2 green onions, ends trimmed, minced
3 cloves garlic, minced
½ teaspoon salt
¼ teaspoon freshly ground black pepper
½ cup chopped fresh basil
1 egg, beaten

ITALIAN TOMATO GLAZE
2 tablespoons olive oil
3 cloves garlic, minced
1 cup bottled tomato or spaghetti sauce
1 cup red wine
2 teaspoons tomato paste
½ teaspoon salt
1 tablespoon minced fresh oregano
½ teaspoon crushed red chile flakes

Prepare the wings for stuffing (see page 7). In a bowl, combine the nuts, veal, red peppers, green onions, garlic, salt, black pepper, basil, and egg. Using your fingers, mix until evenly blended. Transfer the stuffing to a pastry bag and fill the wings.

To make the glaze, place a saucepan over medium heat. Add the olive oil and sauté the garlic until it sizzles, about 1 minute. Then add the tomato sauce, wine, tomato paste, salt, oregano, and chile flakes. Bring to a boil and cook for 10 minutes at a low boil. Cool the sauce to room temperature.

Place the wings in a large bowl and pour the glaze over the wings. Gently coat the chicken wings with the glaze. This can be done up to 12 hours in advance; keep refrigerated.

Preheat the oven to 375°F. Line a shallow baking pan with foil. Coat a wire rack with nonstick cooking spray and place the rack in the baking pan. Drain the wings and reserve the glaze. Place the wings in a single layer on the rack and roast for 45 minutes. Serve.

MEDITERRANEAN PESTO WINGS

Serves 4 as an entrée or 6 to 12 as an appetizer

24 chicken wings
8 cloves garlic, peeled
1½ cups packed basil leaves
1 cup packed mint leaves
½ cup pine nuts, toasted
½ cup extra-virgin olive oil
¼ cup freshly squeezed lemon juice
1 teaspoon salt
1 teaspoon crushed red chile flakes

Cut off the wing tips and save them for making stock. In a food processor, mince the garlic. Add the basil, mint, and pine nuts and mince. Slowly pour in the olive oil, adding enough so that the mixture becomes a paste. Add the lemon juice, salt, and chile flakes, and process again. In a bowl large enough to hold the wings, combine the wings and pesto. Mix thoroughly. Marinate the wings in the refrigerator for 1 to 24 hours (the longer, the better).

If using a gas barbecue or an indoor grill, preheat to medium (350°F). If using charcoal or wood, prepare a fire. When the gas barbecue or indoor grill is preheated or the coals or wood are ash covered, brush the grill with oil, then add the chicken wings. Regulate the heat so that it remains at a medium temperature. Grill the chicken wings for about 30 minutes with the barbecue covered. Turn the wings every 5 minutes. The wings are done when the skin turns an even mahogany color and the meat is tender.

Remove the chicken wings from the barbecue. Cut the wings in half through the joint. Transfer to a platter and serve.

BRAISED CARIBBEAN PIRATE WINGS

Serves 4 as an entrée or 6 to 12 as an appetizer

24 chicken wings

1 cup unsweetened coconut milk

1 cup freshly squeezed orange juice

1 cup chopped fresh pineapple

Grated zest from 1 lime

2 teaspoons Asian chile sauce

1 teaspoon salt

¼ cup chopped mint leaves

2 tablespoons chopped cilantro sprigs

3 tablespoons flavorless cooking oil

4 cloves garlic, minced

2 tablespoons minced ginger

Cut off the wing tips and save them for making stock. Cut the wings in half through the joint. In a large bowl, combine the coconut milk, orange juice, pineapple, lime zest, chile sauce, salt, mint, and cilantro. In a deep 12-inch pan, combine the oil, garlic, and ginger and cook over medium heat. When the garlic begins to brown, add the coconut liquid. Bring to a low boil and add the wings. Cover, turn the heat to low, and simmer until the chicken wings become very tender, about 30 minutes. Stir occasionally. This can be done 24 hours prior to serving.

To serve, bring the wings and sauce to a low boil. Cook until nearly all the sauce evaporates and forms a glaze around the wings. Serve.

Many ingredients combine here to create a dynamic flavor of sweet, sour, rich, spicy, and herbal high notes. It's important to use unsweetened coconut milk, rather than coconut milk used for cocktail drinks, and to avoid "low-fat" coconut milk, which is a grayish color and tastes bad. As for the pineapple, buy the peeled, cored, fresh pineapple sold in small plastic containers.

BRAISED WINGS WITH MEXICAN CHOCOLATE SAUCE

Serves 4 as an entrée or 6 to 12 as an appetizer

24 chicken wings

6 dried ancho chiles

6 cloves garlic, minced

2 cups tomato sauce

2 cups chicken broth

1 cup taco sauce

¼ cup firmly packed brown sugar

1 tablespoon your favorite hot sauce

1 teaspoon ground cinnamon

1 teaspoon salt

½ teaspoon allspice

4 ounces Ibarra Mexican chocolate
or bittersweet chocolate, chopped

¼ cup chopped cilantro or parsley sprigs

Cut off the wing tips and save them for making stock. Cut the wings in half through the joint. Discard the stems and all the seeds from the dried chiles. Place the dried chiles in an electric spice grinder, and grind to a powder. Transfer the powdered chiles to a deep 12-inch pan. Add the garlic, tomato sauce, chicken broth, taco sauce, brown sugar, hot sauce, cinnamon, salt, and allspice. Bring to a simmer and cook at a simmer for 15 minutes. Then add the wings, bring to a simmer, and cook at a simmer until the wings become tender, about 30 minutes. Stir the wings every 5 minutes. This can be done 24 hours prior to serving.

To serve, bring the wings and the sauce to a simmer. Stir in the chocolate. Cook until nearly all the sauce evaporates, about 10 minutes. Transfer to plates or a platter. Sprinkle with cilantro and serve.

GREAT
ASIAN-INSPIRED
WINGS

Unique Flavors from Asian Chefs

ROASTED SZECHUAN WINGS

Serves 4 as an entrée or 6 to 12 as an appetizer

24 chicken wings
1 cup hoisin sauce
¾ cup plum sauce
½ cup thin soy sauce
2 teaspoons grated or minced lime zest
⅓ cup freshly squeezed lime juice
⅓ cup honey
2 tablespoons Asian chile sauce
½ cup chopped cilantro sprigs
6 cloves garlic, minced

Cut off the wing tips and save them for making stock. In a bowl large enough to hold the wings, combine all the remaining ingredients. Add the wings, and mix thoroughly. Marinate the wings in the refrigerator for 1 to 24 hours (the longer, the better).

Preheat the oven to 375°F. Line a shallow baking pan with foil. Coat a wire rack with nonstick cooking spray and place the rack in the baking pan. Drain the chicken and reserve the marinade. Arrange the wings on the rack (smooth surface down) and roast for 30 minutes. Drain the accumulated liquid from the pan. Baste the wings with the reserved marinade, turn them over, and baste again. Roast until the wings turn a mahogany color, about another 30 minutes. Cut the wings in half through the joint. Serve hot or at room temperature.

Thai sweet chili sauce is a sugar syrup infused with crushed red chiles and garlic. It adds a great taste when brushed across chicken or pork tenderloin just minutes before being removed from the barbecue; add it in small amounts to salad dressings, or dilute it with freshly squeezed lime juice to make a dipping sauce for chilled, cooked jumbo prawns.

THAI BBQ WINGS

Serves 4 as an entrée or 6 to 12 as an appetizer

24 chicken wings
1 cup dry sherry or Chinese rice wine
½ cup Thai or Vietnamese fish sauce
1 cup Thai sweet chili sauce
Grated zest of 3 limes
1 cup freshly squeezed lime juice
6 cloves garlic, minced
⅓ cup chopped cilantro sprigs
2 green onions, ends trimmed, minced
2 serrano chiles, minced, including the seeds

Cut off the wing tips and save them for making stock. In a bowl large enough to hold the wings, combine all the remaining ingredients. Add the wings, and mix thoroughly. Marinate the wings in the refrigerator for 1 to 24 hours (the longer, the better).

If using a gas barbecue or an indoor grill, preheat to medium (350°F). If using charcoal or wood, prepare a fire. Drain the wings and reserve the marinade. When the gas barbecue or indoor grill is preheated or the coals or wood are ash covered, brush the grill with oil, then add the chicken wings. Regulate the heat so that it remains at a medium temperature. Grill the chicken wings for about 30 minutes with the barbecue covered. Turn the wings every 5 minutes, basting them on both sides with the reserved marinade. The chicken wings are done when the skin turns an even mahogany color and the meat is tender.

Remove the chicken wings from the barbecue. Cut the wings in half through the joint. Transfer to a platter and serve.

TANDOORI WINGS

Serves 4 as an entrée or 6 to 12 as an appetizer

24 chicken wings
8 cloves garlic
¼ cup thinly sliced ginger
8 dried red chiles, seeded
1 tablespoon whole cumin seeds
1 tablespoon whole coriander seeds
1-inch stick cinnamon
1 teaspoon salt
1 tablespoon ground turmeric
1 tablespoon freshly grated nutmeg
½ to ¾ cup flavorless cooking oil
1 cup unflavored yogurt
¼ cup freshly squeezed lemon juice
¼ cup chopped cilantro sprigs
1 lemon, cut into wedges

Cut off the wings tips and save them for making stock. In a food processor, mince the garlic and ginger. Place the red chiles, cumin seeds, coriander seeds, and cinnamon stick in an electric spice grinder and grind to a powder. Transfer the powder to the food processor, and add the salt, turmeric, and nutmeg. With the processor on, slowly add the cooking oil, and process into a paste; transfer the curry paste to a bowl. Add the chicken wings and rub the curry paste vigorously onto the wings. Marinate the wings in the refrigerator for 1 to 24 hours (the longer, the better). Combine the yogurt, lemon juice, and cilantro and set aside.

If using a gas barbecue or an indoor grill, preheat to medium (350°F). If using charcoal or wood, prepare a fire. When the gas barbecue or indoor grill is preheated or the coals or wood are ash covered, brush the grill with oil, and add the wings. Keep the heat at a medium temperature. Grill the wings for about 30 minutes with the barbecue covered. Turn them every 5 minutes. The wings are done when the skin turns an even mahogany color and the meat is tender.

Remove the chicken wings from the barbecue. Cut the wings in half through the joint. Transfer to a platter and serve, accompanied by the lemon wedges and the yogurt mixture.

This recipe is a great example of why roasting is such a perfect technique for cooking chicken wings. After the first 30 minutes of roasting, the meat is fully cooked, but the skin is still soft-textured and forgettable. It's during the next 30 minutes of roasting that the skin is transformed to a mahogany color and develops a sublime crispness. And amazingly, the wing meat tastes more intensely moist with the extra cooking.

WINGS WITH HOISIN AND RED WINE

Serves 4 as an entrée or 6 to 12 as an appetizer

24 chicken wings
1 cup hoisin sauce
1 cup red wine
½ cup oyster sauce
½ cup freshly squeezed lemon juice
6 cloves garlic, minced
2 serrano chiles, stemmed and minced, including seeds
¼ cup chopped fresh rosemary sprigs

Cut off the wing tips and save them for making stock. In a bowl large enough to hold the wings, combine all the remaining ingredients. Add the wings, and mix thoroughly. Marinate the wings in the refrigerator for 1 to 24 hours (the longer, the better).

Preheat the oven to 375°F. Line a shallow baking pan with foil. Coat a wire rack with nonstick cooking spray and place the rack in the baking pan. Drain the chicken and reserve the marinade. Arrange the wings on the rack (smooth surface down) and roast for 30 minutes. Drain the accumulated liquid from the pan. Baste the wings with the reserved marinade, turn them over, and baste again. Roast until the wings turn a mahogany color, about another 30 minutes. Cut the wings in half through the joint. Serve hot or at room temperature.

93

ROAST WINGS WITH ASIAN PEANUT MARINADE

Serves 4 as an entrée or 6 to 12 as an appetizer

24 chicken wings
1 cup chunky peanut butter
1 cup dry sherry or Chinese rice wine
½ cup dark soy sauce
½ cup wine vinegar (any kind)
¼ cup toasted sesame oil
2 tablespoons Asian chile sauce
6 cloves garlic, minced
¼ cup minced ginger
2 green onions, ends trimmed, minced
¼ cup minced cilantro sprigs
¼ cup finely chopped dry-roasted, unsalted peanuts

Cut off the wing tips and save them for making stock. In a bowl large enough to hold the wings, combine all the remaining ingredients. Add the wings, and mix thoroughly. Marinate the wings in the refrigerator for 1 to 24 hours (the longer, the better).

Preheat the oven to 375°F. Line a shallow baking pan with foil. Coat a wire rack with nonstick cooking spray and place the rack in the baking pan. Drain the chicken and reserve the marinade. Arrange wings on the rack (smooth surface down) and roast for 30 minutes. Drain the accumulated liquid from the pan. Baste the wings with the reserved marinade, turn them over, and baste again. Roast until the wings turn a mahogany color, about another 30 minutes. Cut the wings in half through the joint. Serve hot or at room temperature.

Peanut butter is a great addition to marinades. Not only does it add a fantastic rich taste that appeals to those of us addicted to peanut butter, but it also helps thicken the sauce and thus forms a crustier, more intense layer of flavor on the wings. We prefer chunky, salted peanut butter made from roasted peanuts.

PINEAPPLE TERIYAKI WINGS

Serves 4 as an entrée or 6 to 12 as an appetizer

24 chicken wings

2 cups teriyaki sauce

2 cups pineapple puree (about 8 ounces fresh pineapple
chunks liquefied in a food processor)

2 tablespoons Asian chile sauce or your favorite hot sauce

4 green onions, ends trimmed, minced

¼ cup minced ginger

½ cup firmly packed brown sugar

Cut off the wing tips and save them for making stock. In a bowl large enough to hold the wings, combine all the remaining ingredients. Add the wings, mix thoroughly, and marinate in the refrigerator for 1 to 24 hours (the longer, the better).

Preheat the oven to 375°F. Line a shallow baking pan with foil. Coat a wire rack with nonstick cooking spray and place the rack in the baking pan. Drain the chicken and reserve the marinade. Arrange the wings on the rack (smooth surface down) and roast for 30 minutes. Drain the accumulated liquid from the pan. Baste the wings with the reserved marinade, turn them over, and baste again. Roast until the wings turn a mahogany color, about another 30 minutes. Cut the wings in half through the joint. Serve hot or at room temperature.

One of the classic Cantonese dim sum dishes is steamed chicken wings with black bean seasonings. Here we've modified the recipe so that the wings can be roasted in the oven. A word of caution: some black bean sauces taste very salty. Look for Black Bean Garlic Sauce by Lee Kum Kee.

WINGS WITH CHINESE BLACK BEAN GLAZE

Serves 4 as an entrée or 6 to 12 as an appetizer

24 chicken wings
¾ cup sugar
¾ cup vinegar (any kind)
6 tablespoons toasted sesame oil
6 tablespoons Black Bean Garlic Sauce
6 tablespoons white sesame seeds, toasted
½ cup minced ginger
4 green onions, ends trimmed, minced
2 tablespoons grated orange zest

Cut off the wing tips and save them for making stock. In a bowl large enough to hold the wings, combine all the remaining ingredients. Add the wings, and mix thoroughly. Marinate the wings in the refrigerator for 1 to 24 hours (the longer, the better).

Preheat the oven to 375°F. Line a shallow baking pan with foil. Coat a wire rack with nonstick cooking spray and place the rack in the baking pan. Drain the chicken and reserve the marinade. Arrange the wings on the rack (smooth surface down) and roast for 30 minutes. Drain the accumulated liquid from the pan. Baste the wings with the reserved marinade, turn them over, and baste again. Roast until the wings turn a mahogany color, about another 30 minutes. Cut the wings in half through the joint. Serve hot or at room temperature.

STUFFED WINGS
WITH CHINESE GLAZE

Serves 4 as an entrée or 6 to 12 as an appetizer

24 chicken wings

1 pound ground pork

2 green onions, ends trimmed, minced

2 tablespoons minced ginger

2 cloves garlic, minced

2 tablespoons thin soy sauce

2 teaspoons toasted sesame oil

2 teaspoons Asian chile sauce

2 teaspoons curry powder

CHINESE GLAZE

½ cup hoisin sauce

6 tablespoons plum sauce

¼ cup oyster sauce

2 tablespoons dry sherry or Chinese rice wine

2 teaspoons Asian chile sauce

Prepare the chicken wings for stuffing (see page 7). In a bowl, combine the pork, green onions, ginger, garlic, soy sauce, sesame oil, chile sauce, and curry powder. Using your fingers, mix until evenly blended. Transfer the stuffing to a pastry bag and fill the wings.

To make the glaze, in a separate bowl, combine all the glaze ingredients and mix well. Gently coat the chicken wings with the glaze. This can be done up to 12 hours in advance of cooking; keep refrigerated.

Preheat the oven to 375°F. Line a shallow baking pan with foil. Coat a wire rack with nonstick cooking spray and place the rack in the baking pan. Place the wings in a single layer on the rack. Place the baking pan in the middle of the oven and roast for 45 minutes. Do not baste during cooking. Serve hot.

MAHOGANY WINGS

Serves 4 as an entrée or 6 to 12 as an appetizer

24 chicken wings
1 cup hoisin sauce
¾ cup plum sauce
½ cup thin soy sauce
⅓ cup cider vinegar
¼ cup dry sherry or Chinese rice wine
¼ cup honey
2 green onions, ends trimmed, minced
6 cloves garlic, minced

Cut off the wing tips and save them for making stock. In a bowl large enough to hold the wings, combine all the remaining ingredients. Add the wings, and mix thoroughly. Marinate the wings in the refrigerator for 1 to 24 hours (the longer, the better).

Preheat the oven to 375°F. Line a shallow baking pan with foil. Coat a wire rack with nonstick cooking spray and place the rack in the baking pan. Drain the chicken and reserve the marinade. Arrange the wings on the rack (smooth surface down) and roast for 30 minutes. Drain the accumulated liquid from the pan. Baste the wings with the reserved marinade, turn them over, and baste again. Roast until the wings turn a mahogany color, about another 30 minutes. Cut the wings in half through the joint. Serve hot or at room temperature.

WINGS WITH ASIAN SWEET-SOUR BLUEBERRY GLAZE

Serves 4 as an entrée or 6 to 12 as an appetizer

24 chicken wings
2 cups blueberry or blackberry jam
1 cup wine vinegar
½ cup oyster sauce
¼ cup minced ginger
2 tablespoons Asian chile sauce or your favorite hot sauce
2 green onions, ends trimmed, minced

Cut off the wing tips and save them for making stock. In a bowl large enough to hold the wings, combine all the remaining ingredients. Add the wings, and mix thoroughly. Marinate the wings in the refrigerator for 1 to 24 hours (the longer, the better).

Preheat the oven to 375°F. Line a shallow baking pan with foil. Coat a wire rack with nonstick cooking spray and place the rack in the baking pan. Drain the chicken and reserve the marinade. Arrange the wings on the rack (smooth surface down) and roast for 30 minutes. Drain the accumulated liquid from the pan. Baste the wings with the reserved marinade, turn them over, and baste again. Roast until the wings turn a mahogany color, about another 30 minutes. Cut the wings in half through the joint. Serve hot or at room temperature.

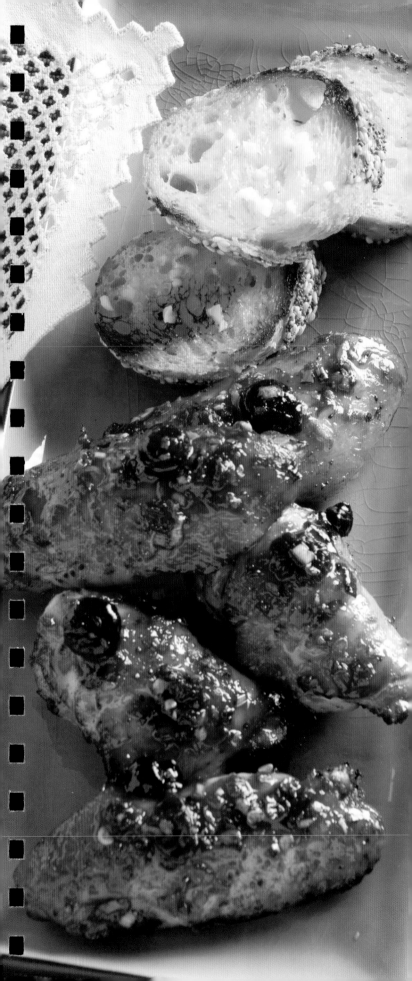

My longtime students will recognize this barbecue marinade. I make it in giant amounts, store it indefinitely in the refrigerator, and use it on everything that's going to be roasted, grilled, or smoked. It makes a wonderful present to distribute during the holiday season or as a fun gift to bring to friends' homes. A word of warning: make the extra effort to buy the brands of Asian seasonings we recommend in the glossary. These are far superior in taste compared to the Chinese condiments manufactured just for American markets.

BBQ CHINESE WINGS

Serves 4 as an entrée or 6 to 12 as an appetizer

24 chicken wings
1 cup hoisin sauce
½ cup plum sauce
⅓ cup oyster sauce
¼ cup wine vinegar
2 tablespoons dry sherry or Chinese rice wine
2 tablespoons toasted sesame oil
1 tablespoon Asian chile sauce
1 tablespoon grated orange zest
1 teaspoon five-spice powder
6 cloves garlic, minced
¼ cup minced ginger
1 green onion, ends trimmed, minced

Cut off the wing tips and save them for making stock. In a bowl large enough to hold the wings, combine all the remaining ingredients. Add the wings, and mix thoroughly. Marinate the wings in the refrigerator for 1 to 24 hours (the longer, the better).

If using a gas barbecue or an indoor grill, preheat to medium (350°F). If using charcoal or wood, prepare a fire. Drain the chicken and reserve the marinade. When the gas barbecue or indoor grill is preheated or the coals or wood are ash covered, brush the grill with oil, then add the chicken wings. Regulate the heat so that it remains at a medium temperature. Grill the chicken wings for about 30 minutes with the barbecue covered. Turn the wings every 5 minutes, basting them on both sides with the reserved marinade. The chicken wings are done when the skin turns an even mahogany color and the meat is tender.

Remove the chicken wings from the barbecue. Cut the wings in half through the joint. Transfer to a platter and serve.

SPICY MANGO WINGS

Serves 4 as an entrée or 6 to 12 as an appetizer

24 chicken wings
2 cups mango puree (from about 4 fresh ripe mangoes)
½ cup freshly squeezed lime juice
3 tablespoons Asian chile sauce
¼ cup oyster sauce
¼ cup honey
6 cloves garlic, minced
¼ cup minced ginger
¼ cup chopped cilantro sprigs or mint leaves

Cut off the wing tips and save them for making stock. In a bowl large enough to hold the wings, combine all the remaining ingredients. Add the wings, and mix thoroughly. Marinate the wings in the refrigerator for 1 to 24 hours (the longer, the better).

If using a gas barbecue or an indoor grill, preheat to medium (350°F). If using charcoal or wood, prepare a fire. Drain the chicken and reserve the marinade. When the gas barbecue or indoor grill is preheated or the coals or wood are ash covered, brush the grill with oil, then add the chicken wings. Regulate the heat so that it remains at a medium temperature. Grill the chicken wings for about 30 minutes with the barbecue covered. Turn the wings every 5 minutes, basting them on both sides with the reserved marinade. The chicken wings are done when the skin turns an even mahogany color and the meat is tender.

Remove the chicken wings from the barbecue. Cut the wings in half through the joint. Transfer to a platter and serve.

BBQ WINGS WITH GREEN CURRY

Serves 4 as an entrée or 6 to 12 as an appetizer

24 chicken wings

8 whole cloves

1 tablespoon black peppercorns

2 tablespoons coriander seeds

1 tablespoon caraway seeds

1 tablespoon cumin seeds

6 cloves garlic, peeled

¼ cup thinly sliced ginger

3 whole serrano chiles, stemmed

3 cups packed fresh basil leaves

1 teaspoon salt

¼ cup flavorless cooking oil

2 limes, cut into wedges

Cut off the wing tips and save them for making stock. Using an electric spice grinder, grind the whole cloves, peppercorns, coriander seeds, caraway seeds, and cumin seeds into a powder. In a food processor, mince the garlic, ginger, and chiles. Add the basil and mince. Add the powdered spices and the salt. With the food processor running, slowly add the oil, stopping when the mixture forms a paste. In a large bowl, combine the chicken wings and the green curry paste. Mix thoroughly, rubbing the green curry paste into the chicken skin. Marinate the wings in the refrigerator for 1 to 24 hours (the longer, the better).

If using a gas barbecue or an indoor grill, preheat to medium (350°F). If using charcoal or wood, prepare a fire. When the gas barbecue or indoor grill is preheated or the coals or wood are ash covered, brush the grill with oil, then add the chicken wings. Regulate the heat so that it remains at a medium temperature. Grill the chicken wings about 30 minutes with the barbecue covered. Turn the wings every 5 minutes. The wings are done when the skin turns an even mahogany color and the meat is tender.

Remove the chicken wings from the barbecue. Cut the wings in half through the joint. Transfer to a platter and serve, accompanied by the lime wedges.

"Curry" means a blend of seasonings and spices ground into a paste. Thai curries have no resemblance to Indian curries, and this is particularly true for this green curry paste, a kind of exotic pesto sauce. When making curry, it's important to use whole spices, such as coriander seeds, because they have a more complex flavor than that of ground spices.

BRAISED WINGS WITH COCONUT CURRY HERB SAUCE

Serves 4 as an entrée or 6 to 12 as an appetizer

24 chicken wings

2 vine-ripened tomatoes, chopped, including seeds

¼ cup chopped cilantro sprigs

1 cup dark raisins

2 cups unsweetened coconut milk

¼ cup Thai or Vietnamese fish sauce

2 tablespoons curry powder

2 tablespoons your favorite hot sauce

1 tablespoon freshly grated nutmeg

2 teaspoons grated orange zest

¼ teaspoon salt

3 tablespoons flavorless cooking oil

2 tablespoons minced ginger

5 cloves garlic, minced

Cut off the wing tips and save them for making stock. Cut the wings in half through the joint. In a large bowl, combine the tomatoes, cilantro, raisins, coconut milk, fish sauce, curry powder, hot sauce, nutmeg, orange zest, and salt. Place a deep 12-inch pan over medium heat. Heat the cooking oil and sauté the ginger and garlic for 1 minute. Add the coconut milk mixture. Bring to a low boil. Add the wings. Bring the liquid to a low boil, cover, turn the heat to low, and simmer until the chicken wings become very tender, about 30 minutes. Stir occasionally. This can be done 24 hours prior to serving.

To serve, bring the wings and sauce to a low boil. Cook until nearly all the sauce evaporates and forms a glaze around the wings. Serve.

ASIAN BRAISED WINGS

Serves 4 as an entrée or 6 to 12 as an appetizer

24 chicken wings
2 green onions, ends trimmed, chopped
2 cups chicken broth
1 cup tomato or pasta sauce
½ cup dry sherry or Chinese rice wine
¼ cup hoisin sauce
¼ cup thin soy sauce
¼ cup oyster sauce
1 tablespoon toasted sesame oil
2 teaspoons Asian chile sauce
3 tablespoons flavorless cooking oil
2 tablespoons minced garlic
2 tablespoons minced ginger

Cut off the wing tips and save them for making stock. Cut the wings in half through the joint. In a large bowl, combine the green onions, chicken broth, tomato sauce, dry sherry, hoisin sauce, soy sauce, oyster sauce, sesame oil, and chile sauce. Place a deep 12-inch pan over medium heat. Heat the oil, then add the garlic and ginger. When hot, add the tomato mixture. Bring the liquid to a low boil. Add the wings. Cover, turn the heat to low, and simmer until the chicken wings become very tender, about 30 minutes. Stir occasionally. This can be done 24 hours prior to serving.

To serve, bring the wings and sauce to a low boil. Cook until nearly all the sauce evaporates and forms a glaze around the wings. Serve.

This is a rich-tasting tomato-based sauce. We have tested this recipe with equally good results using numerous brands of tomato and pasta sauces. As a variation, try boiling the sauce until it thickens, then cool it to room temperature and use it as a marinade for wings before they are roasted in the oven or grilled on the barbecue. Excellent!

BRAISED "RED COOKED" WINGS SHANGHAI STYLE

Serves 4 as an entrée or 6 to 12 as an appetizer

24 chicken wings
2 cups red wine
½ cup dark soy sauce
½ cup firmly packed brown sugar
2 tablespoons hoisin sauce
3-inch stick cinnamon
6 whole cloves
1 teaspoon crushed red chile flakes
¼ cup chopped ginger
6 cloves garlic, minced
1 tablespoon grated orange zest

Cut off the wing tips and save them for making stock. Cut the wings in half through the joint. In a large bowl, combine all the remaining ingredients. Place a deep 12-inch pan over medium heat. Add the red wine mixture and bring to a simmer. Add the chicken wings. Bring to a low boil, cover, turn the heat to low, and simmer until the wings become very tender, about 30 minutes. Stir occasionally. This can be done 24 hours prior to serving.

To serve, bring the wings and sauce to a low boil. Cook until nearly all the sauce evaporates and forms a glaze around the wings. Serve.

Red cooking is a very popular way to cook pork shoulder in the Shanghai area. The pork is simmered for many hours until "chopstick tender" and becomes an amazing glossy reddish color due to the large amount of dark soy sauce used. Wings are also delicious simmered in this manner.

THAI STUFFED WINGS

Serves 4 as an entrée or 6 to 12 as an appetizer

24 chicken wings
1 pound raw shrimp, shelled and deveined
2 green onions, ends trimmed, minced
2 tablespoons minced ginger
2 cloves garlic, minced
2 tablespoons oyster sauce
2 teaspoons Asian chile sauce

THAI GLAZE
⅔ cup Thai sweet chili sauce
¼ cup Thai or Vietnamese fish sauce
1 tablespoon grated lemon zest
½ cup freshly squeezed lime juice
¼ cup minced ginger
4 cloves garlic, minced
¼ cup chopped mint or basil leaves

Prepare the chicken wings for stuffing (see page 7). Finely mince the shrimp. In a bowl, combine the shrimp, green onions, ginger, garlic, oyster sauce, and chile sauce. Using your fingers, mix until evenly blended. Transfer the stuffing to a pastry bag and fill the wings.

To make the glaze, in a separate bowl, combine all the glaze ingredients and mix well. Gently coat the chicken wings with the glaze. This can be done up to 12 hours in advance of cooking; keep refrigerated.

Preheat the oven to 375°F. Line a shallow baking pan with foil. Coat a wire rack with nonstick cooking spray and place the rack in the baking pan. Place the wings in a single layer on the rack. Place the baking pan in the middle of the oven and roast for 45 minutes. Do not baste during cooking. Serve hot.

Lollipop chicken wings are one of the marvels of Chinese cuisine. But it does take practice to make perfect. Since they freeze well, why not spend a morning or early evening making a great mound of lollipop wings that can be stockpiled for future gatherings of friends? Chinese cooks batter and deep-fry lollipop wings, but we think the best technique for home cooking is to rub them with a favorite glaze or barbecue sauce and then roast them in a hot oven. Danny Kaye taught me the lollipop technique in 1979.

CHINESE LOLLIPOP WINGS WITH CITRUS GLAZE

Serves 4 as an entrée or 6 to 12 as an appetizer

24 chicken wings
1 cup hoisin sauce
⅔ cup plum sauce
¼ cup oyster sauce
2 teaspoons Asian chile sauce
3 cloves garlic, minced
1 tablespoon minced ginger

CITRUS GLAZE
2 tablespoons grated orange zest
1 cup freshly squeezed orange juice
¼ cup sugar
½ cup distilled white vinegar
½ cup orange marmalade
¼ cup minced ginger
1 tablespoon Asian chile sauce

Lollipop the chicken wings (see page 4). You should have 48 pieces. In a bowl, combine the hoisin sauce, plum sauce, oyster sauce, chile sauce, garlic, and ginger. Mix well. Dip the lollipop ends into the marinade, then transfer to a shallow baking pan. Marinate for 1 to 24 hours in the refrigerator (the longer, the better).

Preheat the oven to 375°F. Line a shallow baking pan with foil, and spray the foil with nonstick spray. Stand the lollipop wings, meaty end downward, on the baking pan. Place in the oven and roast for 40 minutes.

Meanwhile, make the glaze. In a small saucepan, combine all the glaze ingredients, bring to a boil, and boil until it begins to thicken, about 4 minutes. After the wings are cooked, brush them with the glaze. Serve at once.

CRISPY LOLLIPOP WINGS

Serves 4 as an entrée or 6 to 12 as an appetizer

12 chicken wings
1 tablespoon five-spice powder
1 teaspoon freshly ground black pepper
1 teaspoon salt
2 cups flavorless cooking oil
Your favorite salsa

CHINESE BATTER
1 cup cornstarch
1 cup unbleached white flour
2 tablespoons wine vinegar
1 teaspoon crushed red chile flakes
1 teaspoon salt
½ teaspoon baking soda
½ teaspoon baking powder
2½ cups soda water, chilled

Lollipop the chicken wings (see page 4). You should have 24 pieces. Rub the meat with five-spice powder, pepper, and salt.

To make the batter, in a bowl, combine all the batter ingredients. Stir with a whisk until smooth. Refrigerate the batter until thoroughly chilled.

To cook, place a 12-inch frying pan over medium-high heat on an indoor stovetop or an outdoor gas grill. Add the cooking oil. Heat the oil until bubbles form around the end of a wooden spoon dipped into the oil (350° to 375°F). Stir the batter. Turn the heat to high. Dip the meaty end of 12 wings into the batter and then add to the oil. Deep-fry until the batter becomes deep golden and the meat is cooked along the bone (cut into one with a paring knife). Total cooking time is about 6 minutes. Transfer the wings to a wire rack to drain. Cook the second batch of wings. Serve with your favorite salsa.

There is a famous Vietnamese dipping sauce, nuoc cham, that is used throughout the country to flavor everything from spring rolls to grilled meats and seafood. It's sort of the Vietnamese equivalent of our ketchup, though far more complex-tasting. The dipping sauce ingredients form the foundation for this chicken wing marinade. A word of caution: be sure to buy Vietnamese or Thai fish sauce. Fish sauces manufactured in other Asian countries have a much higher salt content and a stronger taste that will unbalance the flavors in this recipe.

SWEET AND SOUR VIETNAMESE WINGS

Serves 4 as an entrée or 6 to 12 as an appetizer

24 chicken wings
½ cup freshly squeezed lime juice
½ cup firmly packed brown sugar
½ cup Vietnamese or Thai fish sauce
½ cup mango, guava, or papaya nectar
2 tablespoons Asian chile sauce
4 cloves garlic, minced
⅓ cup chopped cilantro sprigs
¼ cup minced ginger
¼ cup minced lemongrass, stem only
¼ cup minced roasted, unsalted peanuts
4 cups shredded iceberg lettuce

Cut off the wing tips and save them for making stock. In a bowl large enough to hold the wings, combine the lime juice, brown sugar, fish sauce, mango nectar, chile sauce, garlic, cilantro, ginger, lemongrass, and peanuts. Add the wings, and mix thoroughly. Marinate the wings in the refrigerator for 1 to 24 hours (the longer, the better).

Preheat the oven to 375°F. Line a shallow baking pan with foil. Coat a wire rack with nonstick cooking spray and place the rack in the baking pan. Drain the chicken and reserve the marinade. Arrange the wings on the rack (smooth surface down) and roast for 30 minutes. Drain the accumulated liquid from the pan. Baste the wings with the reserved marinade, turn them over, and baste again. Roast until the wings turn a mahogany color, about another 30 minutes. Cut the wings in half through the joint. Place a layer of lettuce on a platter. Add the wings on top of the lettuce. Serve.

GLOSSARY

CHILE, ANCHO: These reddish purple dried chiles have a fruity, mild, spicy taste that makes them a particularly great addition to tomato sauces and homemade chili. They are sold in all Mexican markets and American supermarkets that have a wide selection of dried chiles. Substitute: dried mulato or pasilla chiles.

CHILE, FRESH: The smaller the chile, the spicier its taste. More than 80 percent of the "heat" is concentrated in the inside ribbing and seeds. Because it is a tedious operation to remove the seeds from Scotch bonnet, jalapeño, and serrano chiles, we always mince the chiles with their seeds. If recipes specify seeding a small chile, just use half the amount of chile, and mince the chile with its seeds in an electric mini-chopper. Substitute: your favorite bottled hot sauce.

CHILE SAUCES: These are sauces whose primary ingredient is chiles, and are not to be confused with tomato-based "chili sauces." There are countless varieties of chile sauces. Added to provide "heat" to food, use your favorite chile sauce and vary the amount, depending on personal preference. (Make sure you taste it first, before adding to the recipe.) Most of the recipes designate "Asian chile sauce." Our favorite is the Rooster brand of Chili Garlic Sauce, sold in 8-ounce clear plastic jars with a green cap. Refrigerate after opening. Substitute: one or more fresh jalapeño or serrano chiles.

CHIPOTLE CHILES IN ADOBO SAUCE: With a spicy, deep-smoky flavor, these are smoked, dried jalapeños (chipotle chiles) that are stewed in a tomato-vinegar-garlic sauce (adobo sauce). Chipotle chiles in adobo sauce are available in 4-ounce cans at all Mexican markets and many supermarkets. To use, purée the chiles with the adobo sauce in an electric mini-chopper. It is unnecessary to remove the seeds. Substitute: none.

CITRUS JUICE AND ZEST: Freshly squeezed citrus juice has a sparkling "fresh" taste completely absent in all store-bought juices. Because its flavor deteriorates quickly, always squeeze citrus juice within hours of use and keep refrigerated. For recipes that call for "grated zest," remove the colored skin using a microplane rather than trying to scrape the citrus against the fine mesh of a cheese grater (very time-consuming).

COCONUT MILK: This liquid adds flavor and body to sauces. Always purchase a Thai brand whose ingredients are just coconut and water. Do not buy the new "low-calorie" coconut milk, which has a terrible taste. Stir the coconut milk before using. Our favorite is Chaokoh Brand from Thailand. Once opened, store coconut milk in the refrigerator for up to 1 week, and then discard. Substitute: half-and-half.

COOKING OIL: Use any tasteless oil that has a high smoking temperature, such as peanut oil, canola oil, safflower oil, or corn oil.

FISH SAUCE, THAI: Fish sauce, made from fermenting fish in brine, is used in Southeast Asian cooking to add a complex flavor in much the same way that the Chinese use soy sauce. Purchase Thai or Vietnamese fish sauce, both of which have a lower salt content than fish sauce from other countries. Brands we like are Three Crab, Phu Quoc Flying Lion, and Tiparos. Substitutes: thin soy sauce, although the flavor is quite different.

GINGER, FRESH: These pungent and spicy "roots" grown in Hawaii are available at all supermarkets in the produce section. Buy firm ginger with a smooth skin. It is unnecessary to peel ginger unless the skin is wrinkled. Be sure to rinse it thoroughly. Because the tough ginger fiber runs lengthwise along the root, always cut the ginger crosswise in paper-thin slices, then very finely mince in an electric mini-chopper. Store in the refrigerator or at room temperature for up to a month. Substitute: none.

HERBS, FRESH AND DRIED: Fresh herbs have a far more complex flavor than their dried counterparts. The only time we use dried herbs is when they are included in dry rubs. If fresh herbs are not available, substitute 1 to 2 teaspoons of dried for the fresh herbs that are specified.

HOISIN SAUCE: Hoisin sauce, a thick, sweet, spicy, dark condiment, is made with soybeans, chiles, garlic, ginger, and sugar. Once opened, it keeps indefinitely at room temperature. Our favorite brand is Koon Chun.

HOT SAUCE, YOUR FAVORITE: This means use your favorite spicy chile sauce.

LEMONGRASS: Available in most Asian markets, this is one of the most widely used herbs in Southeast Asia. However, the lemon grass sold in markets already has the extremely fragrant green leaves cut off, and the stems are tough and flavorless. Since a lemongrass stalk will develop roots when placed in water or potting soil, grow your own. Use just the leaves, very finely minced. Substitute: an equivalent amount of grated lemon zest, though the flavor is not quite the same.

MUSTARDS, DIJON, CREOLE, HONEY: All types of mustards can be used interchangeably. We prefer Maille brand for Dijon-style mustard, and Zatarain's for Creole-style.

OLIVE OIL: Recipes specifying "extra-virgin olive oil" benefit from this intensely flavored green-tinted oil to add deeper flavor.

OYSTER SAUCE: Also called "oyster-flavored sauce," this condiment gives dishes a rich taste without a hint of its seafood origins, and it keeps indefinitely in the refrigerator. Although it is available at every supermarket, the following sauces, which we prefer, are available mostly at Asian markets: Sa Cheng Oyster-Flavored Sauce, Hop Sing Lung Oyster Sauce, and Lee Kum Kee Premium Oyster-Flavored Sauce. Substitute: none.

PLUM SAUCE: This chutney-like condiment is made with plums, apricots, garlic, red chiles, sugar, vinegar, salt, and water. It is available canned or bottled at all Asian markets and most supermarkets. Our favorite brand is Koon Chun. It will last indefinitely if stored in the refrigerator. Substitute: none.

POMEGRANATE MOLASSES: Much used in the Middle East, this is a thick, very dark syrup, with an intense fruity flavor. Look for this in Middle Eastern markets and gourmet products shops. If unavailable, buy pomegranate juice. Boil in a nonreactive pan until it thickens into a syrup.

POWDERS, GARLIC AND ONION: These are dehydrated garlic or onion flakes that are powdered. Their strong, sharp taste make them appropriate to use only in dry rub mixes, and only in small amounts. If you substitute garlic or onion powder for fresh garlic or onion used in any of the marinades or sauces, the taste of the dish will be ruined.

RICE WINE AND DRY SHERRY: We prefer the flavor of Chinese rice wine. Use a good-quality Chinese rice wine or an American or a Spanish dry sherry. For rice wine, the best ones are Pagoda brand Shaoxing Rice Wine and Pagoda brand Shao Hsing Hua Tiao Chiew, or use a moderately expensive dry sherry. Substitutes: dry Japanese sake or dry vermouth, but not mirin, which is a sweet Japanese cooking wine.

SESAME OIL, TOASTED: A nutty, dark golden brown oil made from toasted crushed sesame seeds, toasted sesame oil should not be confused with the American manufactured clear-colored and tasteless sesame oil, or with Chinese black sesame oil, which has a strong, unpleasant taste. Toasted sesame oil will last for at least a year at room temperature, and indefinitely in the refrigerator. Our favorite brand is Kadoya.

SOY SAUCE, DARK: "Dark," "heavy," or "black" soy sauce is "thin soy sauce" with the addition of molasses and is used to add a rich flavor and color to sauces, stews, and soups. Never confuse "dark" soy sauce with "thick" soy sauce, which is sold in jars and has a syrup-like consistency and an unpleasantly strong taste. Once opened, dark soy sauce keeps indefinitely at room temperature. Our favorite brand is Pearl River Bridge's Mushroom-Flavored Superior Dark Soy Sauce.

SOY SAUCE, THIN: "Thin" or "light" soy sauce is a "watery," mildly salty liquid made from soybeans, roasted wheat, yeast, and salt. If you are concerned about sodium, reduce the quantity of soy sauce, rather than using the inferior-tasting, more expensive low-sodium brands. Our favorite ones are Pearl River Bridge brand Gold Label Light Superior Soy Sauce, Koon Chun brand Thin Soy Sauce, and Kikkoman brand Regular Soy Sauce.

SPICES: Convenience means that most of us use ground, not whole, spices. However, the flavor will be greatly improved if you grind the whole spices into a powder by using an electric spice grinder. Store spices in a cool, dark pantry. Discard whole spices after 2 years, and ground spices after 1 year.

VINEGARS: In recipes that use a certain type of wine vinegar, you can use any type of wine vinegar. In recipes that call for cider vinegar or distilled white vinegar, you can use these interchangeably, or substitute white wine vinegar. For recipes using balsamic vinegar, make the effort to purchase this uniquely flavored nutty, mildly sour, and slightly sweet vinegar. Use the moderately priced balsamic vinegar ($5 for an 8-ounce bottle) available in most supermarkets. If using the mild-tasting Japanese rice vinegar, avoid "seasoned" or "gourmet" rice vinegar, which has sugar and MSG added.

WORCESTERSHIRE SAUCE: This sauce was originally developed by the English in India, and it contains soy sauce, garlic, tamarind, onions, molasses, lime, anchovies, vinegar, and seasonings. It is always available at supermarkets; we prefer Lea & Perrins. Substitute: dark soy sauce.

ACKNOWLEDGMENTS

Many friends helped bring this book into print, and we are deeply appreciative for their support. Thank you, Ten Speed Press, particularly owner Phil Wood, who urged us to do this book. Many thanks also to our editor, Lisa Westmoreland, and to publisher Lorena Jones, who oversaw the entire project.

Special thanks to the endlessly creative ceramic artist Julie Sanders of the Cyclamen Collection. Her beautiful pieces highlight the recipes on pages 41, 48, 57, 66, 75, 82, 106, and 121. Also our thanks to ceramic artist Kathy Erteman for the black and white pieces on page 62.

ABOUT THE AUTHORS

The husband and wife team of Hugh Carpenter and Teri Sandison are the authors of *Fast Fish*, *Fast Entrées*, *Wok Fast*, *Fast Appetizers*, *Hot Wok*, *Hot Chicken*, *Hot Pasta*, *Great Ribs*, *Hot Barbecue*, *Hot Vegetables*, *Quick Cooking with Pacific Flavors*, the *Fusion Food Cookbook*, which received a James Beard Award nomination in 1995, *Chopstix*, which received the IACP nomination for Best Food Photography in 1990, and *Pacific Flavors*, which won the IACP award for Best Asian Cookbook in 1988 and the Who's Who of Cooking Platinum Plate Award for Best Food Photography in 1989.

Hugh Carpenter is one of America's most popular cooking teachers and writers, and his articles appear in many newspapers and leading food magazines. In addition to the cooks he has influenced through frequent television and radio appearances, he has taught more than 100,000 students in classes at cooking schools throughout North America and at his own school in Napa Valley, California, and in San Miguel de Allende, Mexico.

Teri Sandison began her art career in painting and drawing. She then studied photography at the Art Center College of Design, where she specialized in food and wine photography and later was a member of the photography faculty for more than three years. She has done the photography for more than forty cookbooks from leading publishers.

Teri and Hugh live in Napa Valley and in San Miguel de Allende.

INDEX